ALSO BY WILLIAM C. TAYLOR

Practically Radical:
Not-So-Crazy Ways to Transform Your Company,
Shake Up Your Industry, and Challenge Yourself

Mavericks at Work:
Why the Most Original Minds in Business Win
(with Polly LaBarre)

Going Global:
Four Entrepreneurs Map the New World Marketplace
(with Alan M. Webber)

No-Excuses Management:
Proven Systems for Starting Fast, Growing Quickly,
and Surviving Hard Times
(with T. J. Rodgers and Rick Foreman)

The Big Boys:
Power and Position in American Business
(with Ralph Nader)

ABOUT THE AUTHOR

William C. Taylor is the co-founder of Fast Company, author of *Practically Radical* and co-author of *Mavericks at Work*. He has published essays and interviews with CEOs in the *Harvard Business Review*, and blogs regularly for *HBR*. He has written management columns for the Sunday Business section of *The New York Times* and for the *Guardian*. He is a graduate of Princeton and the MIT Sloan School of Management, and lives in Wellesley, Massachusetts, with his wife and two daughters.

@williamctaylor
williamctaylor.com

SIMPLY BRILLIANT

'There's no such thing as an average or old-fashioned business, just average or old-fashioned ways to do business. In fact, the opportunity to reach for extraordinary may be *most* pronounced in settings that have been far too ordinary for far too long'

Far away from Silicon Valley, in familiar, traditional, even unglamorous fields, ordinary people are unleashing extraordinary advances that amaze customers, energize employees and create huge economic value. Their secret? They understand that inventing the future doesn't just mean designing mobile apps and developing virtual-reality headsets.

In *Simply Brilliant*, the visionary co-founder of Fast Company, William C. Taylor, goes behind the scenes at some of the unsung organizations that are revolutionizing their otherwise humdrum fields. These unlikely agents of change range from a parking garage that also serves as a wedding venue to a military insurance company that puts salespeople through simulated overseas deployment.

The message is both simple and subversive: in a time of wrenching disruptions and exhilarating leaps, of unrelenting turmoil and unlimited promise, the future is open to everybody. *Simply Brilliant* illustrates how breakthrough creativity and breakaway performance can be summoned in all industries, if leaders dare to reimagine what's possible in their fields.

PRAISE FOR *SIMPLY BRILLIANT*

'*Simply Brilliant* is, well, simply brilliant! Bill Taylor empowers us with a set of basic, first-order principles in action – on the virtues of kindness, humility and empathy – that turbocharge, and often outdo, all of the more complex ideas we teach in business schools. A must read'

LEN SCHLESINGER, professor, Baker Foundation,
Harvard Business School, president emeritus, Babson College

'*Simply Brilliant* is just that – real examples of the journey from ordinary to extraordinary. Bill Taylor challenges us to think differently about elevating our organizations to be truly distinctive in *what* we do and *how* we do it. His book inspires and equips us to accept that challenge'

SANDRA L. FENWICK, president and CEO,
Boston Children's Hospital

'I have followed Bill Taylor since the early days of Fast Company, and have used some of his ideas myself in the turnaround of Hudson's Bay Company. I'm a strong believer'

BONNIE BROOKS, chief adventurer (vice-chairman), Hudson's
Bay Company (Saks Fifth Avenue, Lord & Taylor, Hudson's Bay)

'The twenty-first-century workplace requires that leaders at all levels become both artists and entrepreneurs. *Simply Brilliant* highlights the power of this creative mix in all kinds of organizations and all sorts of fields. I'll be sharing these stories of original thinking and nimble leadership with my students and colleagues'

TERRI LONIER, dean, career and professional experience,
School of the Art Institute of Chicago

'*Simply Brilliant* is a unicorn among business books: a clear and instructive manual for disruption that also happens to be a terrific read. Bill Taylor has defined parameters for innovation that are relevant and actionable whether your goal is to grow a business or cure a disease'

DEBORAH W. BROOKS, co-founder and executive vice-chairman,
The Michael J. Fox Foundation for Parkinson's Research

SIMPLY BRILLIANT

How Great Organizations
Do Ordinary Things
in Extraordinary Ways

WILLIAM C. TAYLOR

PORTFOLIO
PENGUIN

PORTFOLIO PENGUIN

UK | USA | Canada | Ireland | Australia
India | New Zealand | South Africa

Portfolio Penguin is part of the Penguin Random House group of companies
whose addresses can be found at global.penguinrandomhouse.com

First published in the United States of America by Portfolio/Penguin,
an imprint of Penguin Random House LLC 2016
First published in Great Britain by Portfolio 2016
001

Printed in Great Britain by Clays Ltd, St Ives plc

A CIP catalogue record for this book is available from the British Library

ISBN: 978–0–241–00918–5

www.greenpenguin.co.uk

Penguin Random House is committed to a
sustainable future for our business, our readers
and our planet. This book is made from Forest
Stewardship Council® certified paper.

To Chloe, Paige, and Grace—
you're anything but ordinary

CONTENTS

CONTENTS

PROLOGUE: THE NEW STORY OF SUCCESS

"The Possible Is Immense"

W ho doesn't want to be part of a great success story? To run, start, or play a leadership role in a company that wins big and changes the course of its industry. To launch a brand that dazzles customers and dominates its market. To be the kind of executive or entrepreneur who creates jobs, generates wealth, and builds an organization bursting with energy and creativity.

These days, in the popular imagination, the quest for success has become synonymous with the spread of disruptive technologies and viral apps, with the rise of radical business models and newfangled work arrangements. This is the stuff that fuels the dreams of countless engineers and venture capitalists in Silicon Valley, and inspires hard-charging innovators such as Facebook's Mark Zuckerberg and Uber's Travis Kalanick. The "new economy," the story goes, belongs to a new generation of companies and leaders who have little in common with what came before.

But why should the story of success be the exclusive domain of a few technology-driven start-ups or a handful of young billionaires? The story of this book, its message for leaders who aim to do something important and build something great, is both simple and subversive: In a time of wrenching disruptions and exhilarating advances, of unrelenting turmoil and unlimited promise, the future is open to *everybody*. The thrill of breakthrough creativity and breakaway performance doesn't belong just to the youngest companies with the most cutting-edge technology or the most radical business strategies. It can be summoned in all sorts of industries and all walks of life, if leaders can reimagine what's possible in their fields.

What I have come to understand, what I have tried to bring to life in the pages that follow, is that it is possible to turn even the most familiar offerings in some of the world's most traditional settings into products, services, and experiences that are genuinely remarkable. This is not, I concede, a widely held point of view, even among leaders in those fields. I've heard the same reservations time and again from executives in long-established industries who are reluctant to contemplate a dramatic break from the past: "This place has been around for a hundred years, we're not Google or Amazon," they tell me. Or, "This is not a glamorous business, we can't be a passion brand like Apple or Starbucks."

Their real message: Don't blame me for being average or old-fashioned, I'm not from Silicon Valley or Seattle. To which I reply: Don't use your company's age or industry as an excuse for mediocrity. There is no such thing as an average or old-fashioned business, just average or old-fashioned ways to do business. In fact, the opportunity to reach for extraordinary may be *most* pronounced in settings that have been far too ordinary for far too long. If how you think shapes how you compete, then it should be easier to compete in fields locked in to old ways of thinking.

Why this story now? Because we have entered a new era of business and leadership, an era defined less by advanced technology than by ever-advancing competitive intensity. When customers have higher expectations than ever, when rivals are more capable than ever, when choices, options, and brands are more numerous than ever, then familiar strategies and comfortable ways of working are less effective than ever. In any industry, especially in long-established industries, leaders who make waves and make their mark are the ones who rethink what they've always done, who refresh and reinterpret the products and experiences they offer, who invite new voices into the conversation about the future of their organization.

Why should the story of success be the exclusive domain of a few technology-driven start-ups or a handful of young billionaires?

Thomas L. Friedman, the agenda-setting *New York Times* columnist, has coined a phrase that nicely captures the tenor of these demanding times. "Today," he argues, "average is officially over. Being average just won't earn you what it used to. It can't when so many more employers have so much more access to so much more [above-average] cheap foreign labor, cheap robotics, cheap software, cheap automation, and cheap genius. Therefore, everyone needs to find their extra—their unique value contribution that makes them stand out."[1]

This phenomenon is being played out across the economy and around the world, with huge consequences for those who fail to reckon with it. Lior Arussy, one of the most provocative business thinkers I know, advises some of the world's most prominent companies on the relationship between strategy, innovation, and growth. The problem with most organizations and brands, Arussy likes to say, is not that they are broken. It's that they are *boring*. And boring organizations don't lend themselves to runaway success.

"We are living in a new world," he argues. "Customers no longer accept an 'okay' job. It's exceptional or nothing. In most fields, what was once exciting quickly becomes boring, and boring becomes annoying. 'Impress me, surprise me, do something I will remember'—that's what customers want. That's what organizations have to deliver."[2]

Truth be told, even in a world in which "average is over," the choice facing leaders in most fields is not between one-of-a-kind creativity and end-of-times calamity. The more likely outcome is something closer to endless (and endlessly frustrating) mediocrity. Despite our fascination with digital disruption, radical reinvention, and the merciless logic of survival of the fittest, countless organizations endure for decades in the face of bland results. The status quo is surprisingly powerful, and not always fatal.

"There are many organizations whose performance, by any standard, falls short of the expectations of owners, members, and clients," sociologists Marshall W. Meyer and Lynne G. Zucker remind us, "yet whose existence continues, sometimes indefinitely." In such "permanently failing organizations," their delightfully expressive turn of phrase, executives avoid extinction even as they excite almost no one. The day-to-day reality is one of "sustained low performance" rather than deep-seated crisis, a kind of active inertia driven by short-term self-interest rather than purposeful change driven by a shared drive to excel.[3]

In other words, with apologies to that memorable scene from the movie *Apollo 13*, failure *is* an option, if by that we mean a failure to make the most of the ideas, people, and technologies available to us. This quiet brand of failure—a failure of imagination, a failure of nerve, a failure to muster the will to break from the past—has become a familiar part of the business landscape. Harvard Business School professor Linda Hill, faculty chair of its Leadership Initiative, has argued that run-of-the-mill executives focus on closing "performance gaps"—the difference between what is and what should be. This is the work of efficiency, productivity, improving on the past. But the real action, the true agenda, for leaders is in closing "opportunity gaps"—the difference between what is and what *could* be. This is the work of innovation, transformation, inventing the future. Merely surviving is not the same as truly thriving.[4]

The problem with most organizations is not that they are broken. It's that they are *boring*. And boring organizations don't lend themselves to runaway success.

Simply Brilliant is addressed to leaders who are determined to thrive, not just survive, who aim to write compelling stories of success no matter their industry or field of endeavor. It is organized into four sections, each of which can be read on its own, all of which set out essential principles for exceptional performance—simple, direct, counterintuitive insights that define a new agenda for strategy, innovation, service, and shared prosperity. My hope is that the material is both instructive and inspiring. Instructive in that it delivers a set of messages and lessons that can be applied immediately, inspiring in that it highlights a cast of characters whose ambitions are bold and whose track records are without peer, and who toil in settings that are familiar and relatable.

I traveled thousands of miles during the research for this book, from London, England, to Anchorage, Alaska, from the bright lights of Las Vegas to a quiet town on the banks of the Mississippi River, searching for new kinds of success stories that illuminate the new era we've entered. I spent long days touring factories, visiting retail outlets, and sitting in on meetings to observe the work of big companies, entrepreneurial outfits, nonprofit groups, and social-change movements. These fifteen organizations were from very different fields and had wildly different histories and cultures, but they shared a defining trait: Their leaders were determined to achieve something important by doing even the most ordinary things in extraordinary ways.

I have tried to bring to these stories what John W. Gardner, the legendary public intellectual, called "tough-minded optimism." "The future," Gardner wrote, "is not shaped by people who don't really believe in the future." Rather, it is created "by highly motivated people, by enthusiasts, by men and women who want something very much or believe very much."[5]

Of course, even tough-minded optimists have to face problems, disappointments, crises. That's the pressure that goes with breaking new ground, making big change, doing things that haven't been done that way before. I have no doubt that one or two of the organizations I chronicle will experience setbacks that they (and I) did not anticipate. But what I want very much, what I believe very much, is that the ideas and characters you'll encounter in this book will fuel your enthusiasm to do extraordinary things rather than muddle through in a state of permanent failure.[5]

"The future is not shaped by people who don't really believe in the future." It is shaped "by men and women who want something very much or believe very much."

On one of my last visits for *Simply Brilliant*, I traveled to Euclid, Ohio, a suburb of Cleveland, to spend time with a company I'd been eager to study for years. Lincoln Electric is one of America's great manufacturers, a globally successful producer of welding equipment and cutting machinery founded back in 1895. Lincoln Electric doesn't make many headlines, but it has made history since 1958 by vowing never to lay off a single employee and, since 1934, by sharing a big chunk of its profits with its Cleveland-area employees. In a decidedly unglamorous field, and in the face of recessions, financial collapses, and rapid technology shifts, Lincoln Electric has achieved something unrivaled by recognizing that people are at their most productive when they get a piece of the action and a seat at the table.

As I walked from the corporate offices after a conversation with the CEO to tour the company's massive factory complex, I saw a big sign in capital letters with a message from James F. Lincoln, the younger brother of the company's founder and the visionary behind the company's enduring social system and business model. **THE ACTUAL IS LIMITED**, the sign read. **THE POSSIBLE IS IMMENSE**.

That is the spirit of this book. That is the story of success.

What's your story?

PART I

Stop Trying to Be the Best; Strive to Be the Only

The most successful organizations are no longer the ones that offer the best deals. They're the ones that champion the most original ideas, and do things other organizations can't or won't do.

Chapter 1

WHAT'S YOUR VALUES PROPOSITION?

"Competition Is Not the Same as Choice"

I t's a pleasant, active, fairly unremarkable Friday in Milton Keynes, a pleasant, active, fairly unremarkable city about fifty miles northwest of London, equidistant from Cambridge and Oxford. Milton Keynes offers little of the history, pageantry, and color of these legendary destinations. It is an unassuming place of office buildings, shopping malls, and residential developments—a so-called "new city" created in the 1960s to showcase the power of commonsense urban policies and business-friendly economic strategies. Today, Milton Keynes boasts solid growth and low unemployment, even as it lacks a sense of style. Francis Tibbalds, the late British architect and urban planner, and the author of an influential book called *Making People-Friendly Towns*, was impressed with the substance of what the city had achieved, but dismissed its personality as "bland, rigid, sterile, and totally boring." In a paper titled "Milton Keynes—Who Forgot the Urban Design?" Tibbalds lamented that the city had missed the opportunity "to become one of the world's greatest examples of new place-making" and had become instead "just another collection of good, bad, and indifferent buildings."[1]

All of which makes what's happening in the Oakgrove district so out of character. Crowds of curious residents drive, walk, and otherwise gather around a noisy, energetic sidewalk scene. A DJ is spinning tunes and swaying to the thumping beat of the latest dance music. A clown on stilts is delighting kids and high-fiving anyone tall enough to reach her hand. There's popcorn and ice cream and face painting. There are also several prominent politicians, including the mayor of Milton Keynes, sporting his ornate chain of office, a British ceremonial artifact that extends back to the Middle Ages, and the local member of Parliament, a Tory who beat the mayor in the last election. (The former rivals seem to get along fine.) But perhaps the most notable celebrity is a twelve-year-old Yorkshire terrier named Sir Duffield, who passersby recognize, fawn over, and ask to pet.

Does this energetic gathering herald the opening of a big show from Cirque du Soleil? Or the local premiere of a Hollywood blockbuster? Actually, believe it or not, it's the first day of a two-day festival celebrating the arrival of a new bank—a bank that is taking Milton Keynes, and England as a whole, by storm. Metro Bank opened its first retail location, in central London's Holborn neighborhood, back in July 2010. The company has been on a tear ever since, opening locations in London's busiest areas (Earls Court, Kensington, the City of London financial district), as well as Cambridge to the northeast, Brighton to the south, and Reading to the west. This grand opening is for Metro's second branch in Milton Keynes, and its twenty-seventh in England. The bank's near-term goal is to open 200 locations, sign up 1 million customers, recruit 5,000 employees, and attract $40 billion in deposits by 2020—an audacious plan that has attracted more than $1.4 billion in capital from some of the world's best-known investors and created the buzziest financial-services brand in the United Kingdom.[2]

Metro Bank, it should be understood, is not just another entrepreneurial growth story. It is quite literally unlike any financial institution England has seen before. This location, like all of Metro's retail branches, is bright and brash, playful and provocative. The shimmering glass structure, with its red-and-black interior color scheme, its high ceilings and silver columns, evokes the spirit of a polished Apple Store rather than a musty bank. Signs in the lobby and slogans on the screens of the ATMs feel like rallying cries more than product messages: **LOVE YOUR BANK AT LAST! DOGS RULE! KIDS ROCK! NO MORE STUPID BANK RULES!** Brightly colored coin-counting stations, called Magic Money Machines, look like contraptions Willy Wonka might have designed for his chocolate factory. Images of the company's mascot, an oversized *M* named Metro Man, loom large. (Metro Man himself is on hand to greet the crowd in Milton Keynes.) Bank staffers make their own design statements in keeping with Metro's look and feel. The women wear red dresses with black blazers, or black dresses with red blazers, the men wear suits with crisp white shirts and red ties. Even Sir Duffield sports a fetching Metro Bank dog scarf.

"We didn't come here to make a better bank branch," declares Shirley Hill, the wife of cofounder Vernon Hill and the person most responsible for Metro's "architectural fabric"—a one-of-a-kind blend of physical space, customer experience, and company culture that distinguishes the bank from all of its peers in the United

Kingdom. "We came here to be the greatest in the world. To be a little better is not very interesting, even though it is very easy to do." So what does it take to be the greatest in the world? "It requires fanatical attention to detail," she replies. "Everything we do either helps or hurts the brand. *Everything.* If a sign is crooked, if one of our people doesn't smile, if we don't maintain a sense of energy, then we are hurting the message. We have to make customer service fun for our people. People won't do it if it isn't fun, if they don't feel proud every day. Nobody else works like this."

It's hard to argue the point. For decades, centuries, really, banking in the United Kingdom has been dominated by five so-called high street institutions, the British term for retail banks that accept consumer deposits. The Big Five (giants such as Lloyds, Barclays, and Royal Bank of Scotland) are immensely powerful, highly unpopular, and virtually indistinguishable from one another. A think-tank report from London's Cass Business School estimates that the giant banks account for 77 percent of the United Kingdom's personal accounts and 85 percent of its business accounts, even as the banking system generated 21 million customer complaints from 2008 to mid-2014. The Big Five have struggled under "a toxic culture [that was] decades in the making," the report concludes, with demoralized employees, unhappy customers, and low public esteem. That culture, the think tank warned, "will take a generation to clean up."[3]

"Everything we do either helps or hurts the brand. *Everything.* If a sign is crooked, if one

of our people doesn't smile, if we don't maintain a sense of energy, then we are hurting the message."

Metro Bank is the forward-looking alternative to this tortured history, with an emphasis on history. It is the first new high street bank chartered in England since 1835. Talk about old money: Metro's "youngest" Big Five rival was incorporated before Buckingham Palace became the official home of the British monarch. (Queen Victoria took up residence back in 1837.) No wonder the upstart feels so unorthodox, so full of swagger, so eager to reinvent every aspect of how the industry operates. For example, in a country with a financial system infamous for limited hours and plentiful "bank holidays," Metro locations are open 362 days per year, twelve hours a day during the week, ten hours on Saturday, six on Sunday. (The bank's locations are closed only on Christmas, Easter, and New Year's Day.)

Moreover, in an industry plagued by long lines and painfully slow response times, Metro vows that new customers can walk into a branch, open an account, and leave with a working debit card and full access to online banking—all within fifteen minutes and without any paper forms. It imposes no fees on checking accounts or ATM cards, and makes huge investments in amenities (such as safe-deposit boxes and its coin-counting machines) that have largely vanished from the banking scene in many places. In Slough, a city one hour south of Milton Keynes, Metro opened the first drive-through bank in UK history, an innovation deemed so remarkable (*seriously*) that it attracted the attention of the BBC. In October 2015, when it opened its second drive-through window, this time in Southall, thirty minutes due east of Slough, it created a similar sense of fascination.

But here's what's even more remarkable about the rise of Metro Bank in the United Kingdom. It is, in a real sense, nothing all that new. In fact, it is the living, breathing reincarnation of a business model that Vernon Hill created decades ago in the United States to great acclaim and recognition, and ultimately to great wealth. Hill founded Commerce Bank in 1973, at age twenty-six, with a handful of employees, $1.5 million in capital, and one location in southern New Jersey. Commerce was sold thirty-five years later to Canada's TD Bank for $8.5 billion—after Hill and his colleagues built one of the country's most distinctive financial-services brands, with outposts from Florida to Maine and a major presence in the ultracompetitive New York City market.

"Every great company has redefined the business that it's in," Hill likes to say, and that's what Commerce did up and down the East Coast of the United States. But Commerce didn't rely on cutting-edge technology, never-seen-before business models, or other forms of radical business disruption. Instead, in a bland, dull, colorless field, it created a banking experience around what he calls "retailtainment"—fun, lighthearted, surprising gestures that encouraged customers to visit the branches, spend time there with the kids, and get to know the staffers—rather than treat their bank like the electric utility or the cable company, or, in recent years, to do as many transactions as possible online. Sure, Hill and his American colleagues used to joke that they operated on the "lunatic fringe" of the financial-services industry, that their business practices and culture were so unlike any other bank that their competitors would not dare copy them, even when their results showed how powerful and effective they were. But they were fueled as much by common sense and old-fashioned values as they were by new-wave thinking and futuristic software.[4]

Well, the "lunatic fringe" now extends across the Atlantic. Hill exported the most advanced and cosmopolitan version of the Commerce model, which he and his colleagues rolled out in New York City, first to London and now to cities and towns within a two-hour radius of the British capital. It's hard to overstate the sense of movement and momentum Metro has unleashed. The notoriously skeptical British press has lionized Hill as a breath of fresh air in an industry choking on bad practices and lousy service. When Mike Bird, a reporter covering European markets and financial-services companies, visited Metro's Holborn location to see for himself what the fuss was about, he wrote an article titled "I Was So Impressed with This New British Bank That I Opened an Account." Hill spends a big chunk of his time giving speeches to business leaders eager to learn from his unconventional strategies and brash rules for success. Inexplicably, his canine sidekick, Sir Duffield, has attracted nearly as much coverage as the bank's founder. "Duffy may be the most famous dog since Rin Tin Tin," his proud owner quips as yet another fan asks to pet him. (Hill is only half joking; Sir Duffield has his own business card and Twitter account, along with a stack of newspaper clippings attesting to his celebrity.)[5]

This sense of enthusiasm is not limited to customers and the media. Metro Bank has attracted a genuinely impressive roster of financial backers, from high-powered American billionaires (including hedge-fund titan Steven A. Cohen, home builders Bruce and Robert Toll, and Willett Advisors LLC, which handles investments for Michael Bloomberg) to blue-chip institutional investors such as Fidelity and Wellington Management. In March 2016, less than six years after the bank opened its first location, Hill and Metro Bank announced that they had raised another big round of capital from investors (more than $580 million) and were preparing to be listed on the London Stock Exchange with a market value of roughly $2.3 billion.

Indeed, on the day I visited Metro Bank's London headquarters, one of Hill's early financial backers, a value investor by the name of Thomas Tryforos, happened to be visiting as well. Tryforos, who is a disciple of the security-analysis principles pioneered in the 1930s by Benjamin Graham and David Dodd, and who, like they once did, teaches at Columbia Business School, had never before invested in a new company, which are, by and large, anathema to value investors. "This was the second-biggest investment I ever made, and the first time I invested in a start-up," Tryforos told me. "Now I ask myself, 'Why didn't I make it even bigger?' You can't imagine this until you've seen it yourself. Every person I meet is like a marketing machine for Metro Bank. I went to a branch opening last year and I thought, 'This is my favorite company to visit because it's fun.' And if it's fun for me, as an investor, what must it be like for customers?"

Not to mention employees. Like any fast-growing company, Metro Bank has been on a hiring binge over the last five years, building a team of senior executives, private bankers, commercial lenders, and frontline service people to staff the retail stores. ("Our job is to find great bankers trapped in broken bank models," Vernon Hill quips.) Of course Metro evaluates candidates for their product knowledge, technical expertise, and relevant industry experience, especially as it applies to executives and specialists in commercial banking. But what the bank insists on, explains Danielle Harmer, Metro's chief people officer, is what she calls "zest"—a palpable sense of enthusiasm, a positive energy and sense of commitment to the cause, that informs how people behave, communicate, and interact. "Ultimately, how we treat each other is how we treat our customers," she told me. "So who you are counts for as much as what you know. You can be outwardly zesty or inwardly zesty, either way is fine. But if you're the kind of person who sucks the energy out of those around you, this is the wrong place for you."

In short, in less than six years, Metro Bank has become an undeniable passion brand in a field in desperate need of positive passion. "People here hate their banks," Hill told me in Milton Keynes as he watched the crowd of visitors sizing up his newest location. "In America, people dislike their banks, they find them annoying. This is rabid hate. The high street banks had a cartel. They trained people to accept whatever they offered because they had no alternative. Well, we are the alternative. And customers are going berserk. Everything we did in New York works better in London. Metro will do in ten years what it took Commerce more than thirty years to do."

"KILL ROUTINE BEFORE IT KILLS YOU" —WHY AVERAGE IS OVER

The first rule of strategy is that how you think shapes how you compete. Back in the mid-1980s, a McKinsey & Company consultant by the name of Michael J. Lanning coined a term that still shapes how businesspeople think about competition and markets, and how they evaluate their positioning versus rivals. The true logic of success, Lanning argued, did not just revolve around R&D and the most advanced technology, or supply chains and the most efficient operations—stuff that happens inside the company. Ultimately, success revolved around what happened with customers outside the company, and not just feel-good promises to serve, satisfy, or otherwise delight them. Leaders had to devise what he called a "value proposition"—a "clear, simple statement of the benefits, both tangible and intangible, that the company will provide, along with the approximate price it will charge each customer segment for those benefits." Moreover, organizations had to deliver those benefits on a consistent basis. "Having selected a particular value proposition," Lanning urged, "you must see to it that this proposition 'echoes' throughout the business system to ensure that each activity of the company serves to reinforce the chosen value. New value propositions can certainly lead to a winning strategy, but so can superior echoing of a more ordinary value proposition."[6]

This may not read like a stirring manifesto for strategic revolution, but Lanning's concept of the value proposition galvanized a generation of business leaders around a market-driven agenda of enhancing quality, slashing response times, adding functionality, segmenting markets—delivering features and improvements for which customers were willing to pay. Companies came to understand the virtues of being better, faster, and more reliable, not just because it made their operations more productive but because it made people more eager to do business with them. "All of the company's customers," Lanning advised, "should see significantly more benefit from the transaction than they are being asked to pay." In other words, the way to make sense of competition and markets, to develop long-term strategies that create lasting wealth, was with finely tuned reasoning driven by insights about what customers actually valued.

To which I say yes . . . but. Thirty years after the concept of the value proposition was invented, we live in a world where customers can choose from more options and alternatives than they've ever had, where rivals are more numerous and capable than they've ever been. In this world, success is no longer just about price, performance, features—delivering tangible and rational economic value that responds to what customers need. It is about passion, emotion, identity—sharing a richly defined *values proposition* that revisits basic questions about what customers can expect and what organizations can deliver. The most successful organizations aren't the ones with the most cutting-edge technology or the most radical business plans. They're the ones that champion the most compelling ideas, craft the most memorable experiences, attract the most fervent customers, and recruit the most loyal allies. That is, the organizations that position themselves as an alluring alternative to a predictable (albeit efficient) status quo.

"Most companies aren't dysfunctional, they're dull," argues Lior Arussy, the thinker and consultant we heard from in the prologue. "That doesn't mean they're not innovating, it's that everyone is chasing the same things, and what qualifies as 'standard performance' is always moving up. Success has to evolve to be sustainable. This is not just about strategy, by the way, this is about behavior. You can call a company boring and people don't get offended. But you tell the individuals in that company that they are behaving in ways that are boring, and things get uncomfortable."[7]

Translation: Companies that manage to rise above the pack and stand alone, that win big in fiercely competitive times, are those that create a one-of-a-kind presence and deliver a one-of-a-kind performance that is not just a little better than what other companies do. They do things that other organizations can't or won't do. Vernon Hill is a classic example of an idea-driven entrepreneur who devised a unique values proposition—in his case, to transform a familiar (even "boring") field into a theatrical experience, a way of interacting with customers that customers never asked for until he showed them what was possible. He and his colleagues do things that the other high street banks can't do because they have a point of view about what matters in their field that those banks simply don't recognize.

Put differently, Metro Bank has created what brand strategist Adam Morgan dubs a "lighthouse identity." Morgan is the founder of a global marketing agency called eatbigfish, with offices in London, San Francisco, and New York City. He and his colleagues have spent years studying companies that break from prevailing norms and practices in their fields. These challenger brands, Morgan argues, exhibit many different personalities, from the Democratiser to the Irreverent Maverick to the Feisty Underdog. But all of them exude a strategic presence built on four key pillars. First is a *point of view*: "They have a very particular take on how they see the world." Next is *intensity*: "They offer an intense projection of who they are in everything they do." Then comes *salience*: "They are highly intrusive, one cannot avoid noticing their activity even if not actively looking in their direction." Finally, they are *built on rock*: They assert "a compelling conviction that the stance they are taking is one that is uniquely theirs."

It's this lighthouse identity, their richly defined values proposition, that separates challenger brands from the incumbents in their field, most of whom are content to refine their dollars-and-cents value proposition. Every time you encounter them, however you encounter them, you understand how they see the world and what they care about, why their point of view matters and how they expect to win, and why what they're doing and how they're competing is relevant to you. In short, companies and brands with a lighthouse identity "do not attempt to navigate by the consumer," Morgan argues. "Instead, they invite the consumer to navigate by them."[8]

To be sure, Vernon Hill had access to vast resources that he has used to play for big stakes in and around London, raising huge sums of private capital to establish a one-of-a-kind presence in one of the world's most vital cities. But you don't need deep pockets or marketing glitz to develop a richly defined values proposition. Nor, for that matter, must a lighthouse identity be built first and foremost around a focus on customers. Sometimes, maybe most of the time, entrepreneurs and innovators begin by challenging the expectations of their customers and building an organization that can deliver on a new set of expectations. But they can also begin by challenging the expectations of the organization itself and allowing the people in it to fashion compelling alternatives to a dispiriting status quo.

Organizations with a "lighthouse identity" offer "an intense projection of who they are in everything they do."

Consider the work of a very different European entrepreneur whom I first encountered in the early days of *Fast Company*, and whose company has spent more than two decades breaking new ground in some of the least attractive, lowest-margin businesses imaginable—and building a high-profile, fast-growing, award-winning company in the process. Liisa Joronen, based in Helsinki, created her company and made her name in what is literally a dirty business—cleaning offices, hospitals, and apartment buildings, first in her native Finland and now across much of northern Europe (Sweden, Latvia, Estonia) and even Russia. She started SOL cleaning services (the name SOL is meant to invoke the warmth of the sun) in the early 1990s, carving out a small business unit from one of the oldest companies in Finland, a 150-year-old industrial empire owned by her family. Joronen's father made her CEO of the family business, Lindström, at age thirty-five, but her unorthodox ideas about frontline employees—their capacity to make decisions and govern themselves—clashed with her father's conventional, top-down approach. Rather than cross swords with her father, she spun off one of the company's least-attractive operations and put her ideas to work. And almost immediately, she and her colleagues started to clean up.

Joronen's core insights, which she set out in her doctoral thesis at the University of Helsinki, were as simple as they were profound:

Just because a company like SOL was operating in a low-margin, high-turnover, no-glamour field, it did not have to act that way. It could invent a different way to be in the cleaning business, to elevate the status of the company and everyone in it, based on a new kind of values proposition that applied to employees first and customers second. "Our main goal is to change how cleaners work," she told *Fast Company* just as the company was hitting its stride. "To let them use their brains as well as their hands." The ultimate goal, she declared, is to "Kill routine before it kills you."[9]

Almost nothing about Joronen's company is routine. The personality of SOL headquarters, in a renovated film studio in the middle of downtown Helsinki, is young, playful, energetic. The walls of "SOL City" are painted in bright reds, whites, and yellows. Meeting areas and conference rooms are designed as neighborhoods with unique personalities. Every element of both the building and the culture is built around an over-the-top sense of optimism, good cheer, and an upbeat personality. On Thursdays, for example, SOL offers free soup during lunchtime to all employees and to anyone else who cares to drop in, turning the office into a warm-and-fuzzy refuge in the cold Helsinki winter. Online, to explain itself and its culture, SOL offers a collection of funny, uplifting videos under the theme "Sunshine for your day." (There's also a video of Joronen, in a yellow chicken suit, laughing with colleagues, but as everyone is speaking Finnish, I'm not sure what's so funny.)

But the company's offbeat style isn't truly what sets it apart among its peers. Joronen and her colleagues have built a fast-growing organization by rethinking the very nature of work in a field that few people ever dream of being a part of, but which, like any business, can provide all sorts of opportunities for growth, creativity, and expansion if people are given the chance. That meant distributing decision-making power from headquarters to the field, allowing local teams and offices to set their own business targets and figure out how to meet them, even putting frontline personnel in charge of budgeting, hiring, and negotiating with clients. "Life is hard, work is hard," Joronen told us at *Fast Company*, "but in a service business, if you're not happy with yourself, how can you make the customer happy?"

For example, one of the first innovations that SOL embraced was to insist that its cleaners work during the day, when offices, labs, and hospitals are teeming with people, rather than at night, after most everyone had gone home. What's more, on the job, SOL employees wear bright yellow-and-red jumpsuits, which give them a sense of pride and professionalism and make them impossible for clients to ignore. That in and of itself cuts against the grain of a business where most employees report to client sites after hours, when most everyone has gone home, and conduct themselves as quietly and inconspicuously as possible. But Joronen realized that if her colleagues showed up when their clients were on the job, and conducted themselves in ways that demonstrated their smarts and commitment, clients would ask them to do more. And because local offices and frontline teams were authorized to pitch business and cut deals, cleaners essentially acted as salespeople, not just polishing floors but landing business.

As a result, hospitals that first engaged SOL to clean rooms or change sheets now use its people as nursing assistants, helping patients get to their tests and notifying doctors of emergencies in the rooms. In more and more grocery stores, frontline SOL employees no longer just sweep the floors, they also stock the shelves and update prices. At the Hartwall Arena, home of the Finnish national hockey team, SOL went from cleaning the facility to staffing the information desk to providing security guards to conducting round-the-clock monitoring. In other words, SOL does things that its competitors can't or won't do because it has both strategic aspirations and organizational wherewithal that they simply don't have.

The results speak for themselves. When I first got acquainted with SOL, the company had fewer than 2,000 employees and $35 million in revenue. Two decades later, when I got an update on the business from Liisa Joronen's son, Juhapekka Joronen, who runs a big chunk of the operation, I couldn't help but shake my head at its growth and diversification. At the end of 2015, SOL had more than 11,000 employees, 3,500 of them outside Finland, revenues ten times greater than back in the early days, and entirely new lines of business from security services to a temporary-staffing agency. Liisa Joronen, who has retired from her day-to-day responsibilities at the company, is something of a leadership icon in northern Europe, winning awards, attracting attention from business-school professors, sharing her insights with CEOs from cutting-edge fields eager to learn from SOL's performance in its unassuming field. "People are ambitious and unrealistic," she explained back when the company started out. "They set targets for themselves that are higher than what [we] would set for them. And because they set them, they hit them."

"WE ARE THE ONLY ONES WHO DO WHAT WE DO" —PUZZLES VERSUS MYSTERIES

Over the years, as I've exhorted companies and their leaders to embrace a richly defined values proposition rather than a dollars-and-cents value proposition, I've heard all kinds of warnings about the downside to thinking bigger and aiming higher. One common worry is the inevitable competitive backlash: If a braver, more clever, more forward-looking company succeeds at doing something new, the reasoning goes, then surely larger, richer, more established companies will decode that success, mimic its logic, and upend the innovator who moved first. What's the point of launching a whole new way to be in a business if you are inevitably going to be shot down by rivals with all the strategic firepower they need?

Think about Microsoft's legendary (and lethal) response to Netscape, the Silicon Valley start-up that released the first popularly available Web browser and ushered in the Internet revolution—only to be crushed by a copycat browser from the software giant a few years later. Or how the cable titans co-opted the breakthrough recording-and-playback technology pioneered by TiVo, which forever changed how all of us watch television, even as it left TiVo a pale shadow of its one-time aspirations for glory. In life, Clare Boothe Luce famously quipped, "No good deed goes unpunished." In competitive strategy, the worry goes, "No good idea goes uncopied."

Were that the case! In the real world, the struggles of promising game changers such as Netscape and TiVo look more like the exception than the rule, cautionary tales that can inspire far too much caution in a world starved for originality and imagination.

Indeed, I'm constantly amazed at how unwilling or unable most big, incumbent, long-established organizations are to learn from (let alone copy) the market makers in their field. Imitation may be the sincerest form of flattery, but it's among the rarest forms of competitive response. And it's certainly no excuse for limiting, in advance, the scope of your strategic ambitions. What your competitors *won't* do, despite how much they know about what you're doing, may surprise you.

There's a reason for that. More than a decade ago, a national security expert by the name of Gregory Treverton made an important distinction about gathering intelligence that prompted many U.S. government agencies to rethink how they evaluated rivals and sized up threats. His distinction, it turns out, also explains why the companies we've visited are so hard for their rivals to evaluate. During the Cold War, Treverton argues, the questions intelligence agencies faced were *puzzles*: How many weapons were in the Soviet arsenal? Did China sell missiles to Pakistan? Today, the most important questions are *mysteries*: Why would Saddam Hussein boast about weapons of mass destruction that he did not possess? Will Iran live up to its nuclear agreements with the West?

What's the difference between a puzzle and a mystery? Puzzles, Treverton explains, can be solved with better information and sharper calculations. Mysteries, however, can only be framed, not solved. "A mystery is an attempt to define ambiguities," he writes. "Puzzles may be more satisfying, but the world increasingly offers us mysteries." And treating mysteries like puzzles, he warns, can be dangerous and delusional—creating a false sense of confidence that crunching more information will clarify situations that can be understood only with more imagination.[10]

Well, what's true for intelligence gathering is also true for thinking intelligently about strategy and competition. As puzzles, the companies we've met don't have many missing pieces. There's nothing about savings accounts or office-park cleaning that can be patented, no "intellectual property" that can be hidden from prying eyes. There's also nothing very secretive about the processes behind the products. Vernon Hill is happy to share the Metro Bank model with entrepreneurs eager to learn from him, and Liisa Joronen and her colleagues advocate for what they call the SOL Operating System whenever they can. So the reason these companies are so distinctive is not because other companies lack the information to mount a challenge. It's because they lack the imagination to match and respond to these "lighthouse" competitors, to summon their passion and patience for doing business their way. To their competitors, companies like Metro Bank and SOL remain mysteries— one-of-a-kind organizations built on principles that they simply can't imagine replicating.

What your competitors *won't* do may surprise you. Don't let worries about imitation limit your enthusiasm for innovation.

The unchallenged rise of Metro Bank in London may be the ultimate case in point. From the moment Vernon Hill announced his intention to enter the UK market, the high street establishment knew what it was in for. His strategic playbook was an open book for any powerful organization that wished to copy it, or at least respond to it. Hill made no secret of the business model he planned to roll out in London (he spent years in discussions with regulators to get their approval), and the performance of Commerce Bank in the United States was well-known and well documented, including in the form of a widely read Harvard Business School case study. Some time-traveling Paul Revere in reverse could have galloped down Oxford Street or around Piccadilly Circus shouting, "Vernon Hill is coming! Vernon Hill is coming!"

So how did the Big Five respond? With a big whiff. In fact, it was precisely this lack of response that allowed Hill to recruit Metro Bank's CEO, Craig Donaldson, who has been instrumental since the earliest days of its meteoric growth. Donaldson was an up-and-coming executive at the Royal Bank of Scotland, a thirtysomething leader responsible for a business unit with ten thousand people and billions of dollars in revenue, when he was sent to Harvard Business School for an executive education program. Lo and behold, one of his first assignments was the Commerce Bank case. What Donaldson learned startled him, intrigued him, made him think. After he returned to London, he was asked to strategize about RBS's future retail-banking presence in the United Kingdom. So he went back to the United States, this time to see Commerce for himself. (By this point, Commerce had been sold to TD Bank, but the core ideas were still in place.) He grew more enthusiastic than ever, convinced that RBS could reclaim lost ground if it adopted some of the practices that made Commerce so successful. Donaldson made his pitch to the board, but it was rejected in favor of recommendations from (fittingly enough) McKinsey, which advised RBS to cut costs, close branches, reduce head count, and emphasize online banking.

"At that time, all the big banks were going in the same direction," Donaldson recalls during a break in the branch-opening festivities in Milton Keynes. "Everybody was cutting costs and closing locations. I'm a great believer that if everyone is heading in one direction, you should head in the other. Zig when others are zagging." Alas, there would be no zigging in Donaldson's future—until, shortly after the board decision, he got a call from Vernon Hill, who was looking for an experienced (and open-minded) London banker to help lead his British invasion. Donaldson, amazed by the timing of the call, told Hill that he had already studied his operation in the United States and had recommended that RBS embrace it. "If you can't copy the bank," the American replied, "why don't you come talk to me about setting it up in Britain?"

Thus began a series of transatlantic trips, including long stays at Hill's vast estate in Moorestown, New Jersey, during which he and Hill would talk strategy, visit banks and other retailers, and develop a shared mind-set about what Hill wanted to build in the United Kingdom. (Nothing Vernon and Shirley Hill do, it should be said, qualifies as average. Their Moorestown home, called Villa Collina, or "Hill House" in Italian, is a granite-clad Italianate palazzo that sits on forty-four acres and features waterfalls, sculpture gardens, and a "lemon room" with a variety of trees.) Donaldson was impressed by both the surroundings and the business strategy, but most of all by what he calls Vernon Hill's "zealot-like focus on the customer." Still, it was an unexpected encounter at the Philadelphia International Airport that ultimately convinced him to sign on as Metro's CEO.

"The last time I flew in to see Vernon, there was this big guy behind the counter at passport control," he says. "These guys never smile, they never make personal conversation. He looks at my passport and says, 'Sir, this is the fourth time you've been in the country in the last few months, can you explain why?' I tell him that I am here being interviewed for a job to set up a new bank, working with a local fellow named Vernon Hill. 'What?' he says. 'Vernon is setting up a new bank?' Then he turns to the guy behind the glass. 'Ralph, Vernon Hill is setting up a new bank! The power of red! It hasn't been the same since it went green!' [TD Bank's corporate color is green, as opposed to the red used by Commerce and now Metro.] Then I thought, how do I break it to these guys that the bank we're setting up is in England? I got in the car after I cleared customs, rang up my wife, and told her I had to take the job. I had never seen anything like that in my life."

Those passport-control officers didn't express unbridled enthusiasm about something as mundane as a bank because Vernon Hill's outfit was a little friendlier or a little more convenient than other banks. It was because Hill and his colleagues had created a way of being in the business, a sense of energy and color, that simply did not exist anywhere else. They made promises other banks could not make: unprecedented hours, unusual services, unique terms and conditions for normally cookie-cutter products such as checking accounts and debit cards. They delivered a performance no other bank could deliver, from stylish facilities to silly mascots to cheerful employees. All of which makes it so disconcerting, in the United States or the United Kingdom, for banks that have been around for centuries to respond in meaningful ways.

"If a typical British banker thought about starting something like this, he'd get ten friends together, they'd hire ten consultants, and they'd come up with a hundred reasons why it wouldn't work,"

Vernon Hill cracks. "The big banks can see what we are doing, but when they run it through their models, do the usual ROI analysis, they can't figure out how it works. Competing like this requires a leap of faith. That's why most things are so bland. Nobody is willing to take a leap of faith."

That's precisely what CEO Craig Donaldson experienced up close and personal when he was an executive at RBS, and how his big-bank rivals are responding (or failing to respond) to the Metro challenge today. "Go look at the established banks," Donaldson says. "They are all competing to do the same things. Lloyd's is green, Barclays is blue, but it's the same products in the same stores with the same hours. Same, same, same. That may be competition, but it's not choice. We bring choice. Competition is not the same as choice."

Shirley Hill explains Metro's unusual and uncopied presence even more simply. "We don't exist for us, we exist for the customer," she says, as she and Sir Duffield take one last tour of the Milton Keynes operation. "Everything we do is designed to make the customer happy, to look for reasons to say yes. This message, this attitude, this culture, is a way of life. It's amazing how many of our people will visit other banks, take pictures, and send them to me—'Can you believe how terrible this is?' I truly think we are the only ones who do what we do."

Chapter 2

WHY MISSIONARIES BEAT MERCENARIES (AND PASSION BEATS DRIVE)

"Some Things Have to Be Believed to Be Seen"

A few years ago, *Fortune* editor Adam Lashinsky wrote a well-reported book called *Inside Apple* that offered lots of intriguing material about Steve Jobs and the strategic choices, design principles, and business tactics that gave rise to a juggernaut unlike any the business world has seen. The book more than lives up to its title. There are colorful details on Apple's obsession with secrecy and the extraordinary lengths to which the company went to keep new projects under wrap from outsiders (and even company insiders). There's an eye-opening chapter, titled "Overwhelm Friends/Dominate Foes," about the demanding ways in which Jobs and Apple dealt with partners and competitors. There is a nuanced analysis of Apple's commitment to design and the exacting level of detail that attaches to even the tiniest elements of the company's product and packaging.

But for all of Lashinsky's behind-the-scenes stories about Apple's legendary founder, it was a public story about Jobs's successor,

CEO Tim Cook, that offered a truly powerful insight for market makers everywhere. The story goes back to Cook's initial conference call with Wall Street after Jobs announced his medical leave of absence. The first question, Lashinsky reports, was from an analyst who wanted to know how the company would be different if Cook replaced Jobs permanently, which, of course, he eventually did. Cook did not respond with a detailed review of Apple's technologies, products, or retail presence—what it sold. Instead he offered a statement of what he and everyone else at Apple *believed*, "as if reciting a creed he had learned as a child" in Sunday school.

"We believe that we are on the face of the earth to make great products, and that's not changing," Cook declared. "We believe in the simple not the complex. . . . We believe in saying no to thousands of products, so that we can really focus on the few that are truly important and meaningful to us. We believe in deep collaboration and cross-pollination of our groups, which allow us to innovate in ways others cannot. And frankly, we don't settle for anything less than excellence in every group in the company, and we have the self-honesty to admit when we're wrong and the courage to change. And I think that regardless of who is in what job those values are so embedded in this company that Apple will do extremely well. . . . I strongly believe that Apple is doing the best work in its history."[1]

For companies and brands that aspire to do something truly extraordinary, what you believe has become as important as what you sell. The job of leadership today, the essence of strategy and competition, is about more than introducing marginally superior products or providing better-than-average service. It is about developing a set of deeply held principles that challenge received wisdom, and helping your organization get to the future first. Simon Sinek has written that great leaders "Start with Why"—they "choose to inspire rather than manipulate" and to "rally those who believe" to support a shared cause. He's right. Whatever the specifics of the company or the field, leaders who break new ground are those who are willing to make promises that other leaders won't make, because they have a point of view about the future that other leaders don't share. As the English poet Ralph Hodgson put it, "Some things have to be believed to be seen."[2]

For companies and brands that aspire to do something extraordinary, what you believe has become as important as what you sell.

John Doerr, the chairman of Kleiner Perkins Caufield & Byers, and one of the world's most accomplished venture capitalists, makes a poetic distinction of his own between two kinds of entrepreneurs and company builders—a distinction that gets to the heart of the difference between competing on what you sell rather than on what you believe. The definition of an entrepreneur, Doerr likes to say, is someone who "does more than anyone thinks possible with less than anyone thinks possible." And successful entrepreneurial ventures, whatever their industry or discipline, share a number of important traits: an A+ founder or founding team, a commitment to technical excellence, a devotion to building an authoritative, trusted brand and an obsession with the customer experience, a reasonable approach to financing, and a sense of urgency.[3]

But the most important trait, the distinction that separates high-impact entrepreneurs from those who don't make such a big difference, is less about what they do and more about what they believe and how they behave. The company builders Doerr is most eager to work with are "missionaries." The others, the ones he finds less compelling, are "mercenaries." There is room for both kinds of leaders, he concedes, but the difference between mercenaries and missionaries "is all the difference in the world."

In Doerr's mind, mercenaries are "opportunistic." They're "all about the pitch and the deal" and eager to sprint for short-term payoffs. Missionaries, on the other hand, are "strategic." They're all about "the big idea" and partnerships that last, they understand that "this business of innovation is something that takes a long time"—a marathon. Mercenaries have "a lust for making money," while missionaries have "a lust for making meaning." Mercenaries obsess about the competition and fret over "financial statements," while missionaries obsess about customers and fret over "values statements." Mercenaries display an attitude of entitlement and revel in the "aristocracy of the founders," while missionaries exude an attitude of contribution and welcome good ideas wherever they originate. Mercenaries strive for success; missionaries aspire to "success and significance."

Ultimately, Doerr argues, drawing on a distinction first made by entrepreneur and author Randy Komisar, himself a Kleiner Perkins partner, mercenaries are motivated by "drive," while missionaries are motivated by "passion." What's the difference? "Passion and drive are not the same at all," Komisar explains in his influential book, *The Monk and the Riddle*, which has become a bible of sorts for Silicon Valley entrepreneurs who aspire to create tremendous value without losing their values in the process. Drive, he says, "pushes you toward something you feel compelled or obligated to do." Passion "pulls you toward something you cannot resist." It comes down to who you are and what you believe. "If you know nothing about yourself, you can't tell the difference," Komisar says. "Once you gain a modicum of self-knowledge, you can express your passion."[4]

An entrepreneur "does more than anyone thinks possible with less than anyone thinks possible."

That's a lofty ambition, I suppose, but it speaks to a lesson I've learned and relearned as I've studied hugely successful innovators in brutally competitive industries. And it's a lesson, oddly enough, expressed most lyrically in a tribute to another California institution, the Grateful Dead rock band. The Dead hold an iconic spot in the history of popular music thanks to their unique sound, devoted fan base, and ahead-of-its time business model that generated almost all of the group's revenue from live performances rather than studio recordings—a model that musicians and executives still learn from today.

Talk about a long, strange trip: The Grateful Dead have gone from symbols of the counterculture to fodder for marketing case studies and meditations on the nature of creativity. One business-school professor, an authority on executive leadership and a veteran of IBM and John Deere, actually wrote a book called *Everything I Know About Business I Learned from the Grateful Dead*, which identifies lessons from the band's creativity and staying power that can inspire other organizations. The book has inspired a cottage industry of journalists, marketers, and business analysts eager to turn their youthful indiscretions into management wisdom.

"By implementing a loose management style, long on flexibility and short on structure, the Dead pioneered practices and strategies that would subsequently be embraced by corporate America," argues Barry Barnes. "They placed an enormous value on customer service, and understood that keeping customers happy led to greater profitability. . . . Throughout all their ups and downs, they remained committed to improvisation and innovation, and they were never satisfied unless they were constantly reinventing themselves, their music, and their business. In today's business climate, beset by crisis and continual change, what lesson could be more important?"

Back in the early days, when the band was at the height of its powers, Bill Graham, the legendary rock promoter, himself an entrepreneur of the first order, was asked why the Grateful Dead were so successful. He didn't talk about their songs, their tours, or how their approach to the music business was a little more progressive than everyone else's—their drive. He talked about the band's sense of mission and purpose, what they were trying to achieve without regard to how anyone else operated—their passion. "They're not just the best at what they do," Graham said. "They're the only ones who do what they do."[5]

I can't think of a more compelling way to describe the mind-set, the outlook, the point of view, required to achieve something extraordinary in highly competitive fields, whether it's the business of filling stadiums with music fans or the challenge of building organizations that will thrive, not just survive, in a turbulent world. As a company or as an individual, the goal is no longer to be the best at what lots of other people do. It's to be the only one who does what you do. That is, to approach your work, your company, your style of leadership, as a missionary rather than a mercenary.

"IF WE CHASE PERFECTION WE CAN CATCH EXCELLENCE" —EXTRAORDINARY PERFORMANCE IN ORDINARY SETTINGS

In his three-plus decades as a venture capitalist, John Doerr has funded some of the best-known business missionaries in some of the world's most advanced and dynamic fields, from life sciences to ecommerce to mobile apps. But Doerr's critical distinction doesn't just apply to high-flying, world-shaking innovators based in San Francisco or Seattle. The virtues of missionaries over mercenaries, the impact of passion as opposed to drive, apply to fields with none of the star power of smartphone technology or the cultural cachet of social media. That is one of the messages at the heart of this book: You don't have to be in a cutting-edge business to develop some edgy ideas on how to compete and win.

Are you hungry for evidence that it is possible to do extraordinary things in some pretty ordinary settings? Then head to Kingsport, Tennessee, pull into Pal's Sudden Service, and order a Sauceburger, large Frenchie Fries (yes, I got that right), and a sweet tea, the most popular item on the menu. You'll leave with a mouthwatering (if highly caloric) meal, plenty of time to eat it, and lots of food for thought about the big lessons this small company has to offer. Over the years I've come to appreciate that you often discover the most amazing ideas in the most unexpected places. Pal's is one of those places. What you learn here will stick to your ribs, and feed your appetite to learn more.

At first blush, there's nothing all that amazing about Pal's Sudden Service. It has twenty-eight locations in northeast Tennessee and southwest Virginia, all within an eighty-mile radius of its home base in Kingsport, in what's known as the Mountain Empire region, nestled between the Appalachians and the Great Smoky Mountains. It sells hamburgers, hot dogs, chicken sandwiches, fries, shakes—pretty much standard fast-food offerings, although the taste and quality have a well-deserved reputation for excellence. (Having sampled the fare, I still get the occasional craving for the Frenchie Fries, which are truly without peer.) Dig deeper, though, and you begin to appreciate that nothing about Pal's is standard for its business—or any business.

What makes the company so special? Most obvious is its fanatical devotion to speed and accuracy. Pal's does not offer sit-down service inside its restaurants. Instead, customers pull up to a window, place their orders face-to-face with an employee (no scratchy loudspeakers), pull around to the other side of the facility, take their bag, and drive off. All this happens at a lightning pace—an average of eighteen seconds at the drive-up window to place an order, an average of twelve seconds at the handout window to receive the order. That's *four times faster* than the second-fastest quick-serve restaurant in the country, which requires more than a minute on average to take an order. (Hence the name, by the way. When Fred "Pal" Barger founded the company decades ago, he wanted to communicate that his outfit would dramatically outperform traditional fast food. What's faster than fast? *Sudden* service. The company's slogan: "Great food in a flash.")

But Pal's is not just absurdly fast—sorry, sudden. It is also staggeringly accurate. You can imagine the opportunities for error as cars filled with bickering families, rowdy teenagers, or frazzled businesspeople zip through the double-drive-through stations in fewer than twenty seconds. ("I said Sausage Biscuit, not Gravy Biscuit"; "I wanted a Double Big Pal, not a Double Big Pal with cheese.") Yet Pal's makes a mistake only once in every thirty-six hundred orders. That's *ten times better* than the average fast-food joint, a level of near perfection that is without peer in the business. Indeed, one reason customers pull away from the handout window in twelve seconds or fewer is that almost none of them bother to check their orders before they drive off. It is the universal mantra of the Pal's experience: "We don't look in the bag because we know it's right." Says David Jones, an instructor at the Pal's Business Excellence Institute (more on that later): "It is not acceptable to us that a customer gets his or her order wrong—*ever.* There is a huge difference between doing it right most of the time and all of the time. We expect all of the time."[6]

Don't get the wrong idea. Pal's is not some sort of robotic assembly line churning out orders quickly, accurately, and colorlessly. There is a real sense of whimsy about the restaurants. Their vivid blue exteriors and stair-stepped designs feature giant statues of burgers, hot dogs, fries, and a drink cup. When I pulled up for the first time, I couldn't resist the urge to park the car, jump out, and persuade someone to snap a photo of me in front of the place. (Sadly, my selfie skills are not exactly world-class.) A huge sign outside each location displays a new **THOUGHT OF THE DAY** every day, and these gems of insight and inspiration ("Chase Your Dream," "Wave at a Policeman") get posted to the company's Web site and Facebook page. The menu is limited and pretty fixed, the better to deliver speed and accuracy. But Pal's also spices up its menu with goofy-sounding limited-time offers, like the Bar-B-Dog (pulled pork on a hot dog bun) and the self-explanatory Lil' Philly Steak Melt. Hard-core customers also know that there are a bunch of "secret" menu items that represent strange and offbeat variations on the formal offerings but never appear in public.

The result of this relentless efficiency and colorful personality—a true lighthouse identity, to use Adam Morgan's phrase—is a level of customer loyalty that is off the charts for the quick-serve field. One trade magazine claimed that Pal's is "loved with cult-like ardor" in the places it operates, and it's no exaggeration. Pal's customers visit its restaurants an average of three times per week. McDonald's customers, by comparison, visit its restaurants an average of three times per month. I make no claims about the health consequences of all this repeat business, but the financial consequences are clear. An individual Pal's location, which requires only 1,100 square feet of space, generates a staggering $2 million of annual revenue, a sales-per-square-foot performance ($1,800) that is the envy of just about any fast-food restaurant in America. (The typical McDonald's location generates less than $650 of annual sales per square foot.)

These facts and figures speak only to bottom-line results.

What's truly intriguing about Pal's, though, is the level of intelligence and intensity with which it approaches everything it does—how it hires, how it trains, how it shares its ideas with other companies eager to learn from its success. Despite the rather humble field in which it operates, Pal's Sudden Service ranks among the most committed, the most reflective, and the most *intellectual* companies I have encountered. But don't take my word for it. Back in 2001, Pal's became the first restaurant company of any kind to win the prestigious Malcolm Baldrige National Quality Award—an award that's been won over the years by Cadillac, FedEx, and Ritz-Carlton. Since then, only one other restaurant company has won a Baldrige—and that company, it would be the first to admit, learned everything it knows by studying Pal's.

"If you watch professional athletes, everything they do looks so smooth and fluid," says Thomas Crosby, who joined Pal's in 1981 and became CEO in 1999. "But eventually you realize how much work went into that performance, all the training, all the skill building, all the hours. It's the same for us. We are known for speed, but there are no timers in any of our restaurants. We are very particular about process design, quality, hiring, and training. We home in on the key elements of the customer experience, the things we can be great at, and work on them until everyone can be smooth and fluid. Speed is the outcome, but it's not the point of the exercise."

So what *is* the point of the exercise, the big-picture mission that drives this quick-serve outfit and allows it to connect so personally with customers who never sit down inside its locations and have interactions with frontline employees that, by design, last for only a matter of seconds? "Customers don't come here to spend time with us," Crosby replies. "They want us to make their lives a little easier. They're in such a hurry, they have so much else to do, we help them get on with their lives. And we treat them like adults—there's no 'suggested selling,' no 'Would you like a drink with that?' Our customers know what they want, they don't need us to suggest extras. So we give you back your time. And we give you the confidence that when we hand you that bag, everything is just as you asked for it. You hit the accelerator and you're on your way."

It's hard to capture just how much careful thought Pal's applies to the seemingly mundane task of making burgers and fries quickly and well, or just how personally Thom Crosby and his colleagues take their work. But here's a little taste of how the company runs. Pal's twenty-eight locations employ roughly 1,020 workers, 90 percent of whom are part time, 40 percent of whom are between the ages of sixteen and eighteen. The company has developed and fine-tuned a screening system to evaluate candidates from this notoriously hard-to-manage demographic—a sixty-point psychometric survey, based on the attitudes and attributes of Pal's star performers, that does an uncanny job of predicting who is most likely to succeed at the company. Among the agree–disagree statements: "For the most part, I am happy with myself"; "I think it is best to trust people you have just met"; "Raising your voice may be one way to get someone to accept your point of view."

Once Pal's selects its candidates, it immerses them in massive amounts of training and retraining, certification and recertification. New employees get 120 hours of training before they are allowed to work on their own, and must be certified in each of the jobs they do: grilling burgers, making fries, mixing shakes, taking orders. (Most employees are certified in as many as eight different jobs, although some specialize in just one or two.) Then, every day on every shift in every restaurant, a computer randomly generates the names of two to four employees to be recertified in one of their jobs—pop quizzes, if you will. They take a quick test, see whether they pass, and if they fail, they get retrained for that job before they can do it again. (The average employee gets two or three pop quizzes per month.) The goal is for everyone at the company to be so good at what he or she does, to stay at the top of their game throughout their tenure at Pal's, that the company operates at what it calls the Triple 100—100 percent execution 100 percent of the time, even when restaurants are operating at 100 percent of capacity.

It's like that maxim from legendary football coach Vince Lombardi: "Perfection is not attainable, but if we chase perfection we can catch excellence." CEO Thom Crosby puts it slightly differently: "We believe in certification over graduation," he explains. "We train you, we graduate you—that's when most companies stop. But people go out of calibration just like machines go out of calibration. So we are always training, always teaching, always coaching." Importantly, Crosby adds, most of that coaching is built around positive reinforcement for superior behavior, "catching people in the act of doing it right." At Pal's, "If people aren't doing something right, that's not a problem with them, it's a problem with the training. We are cheerleaders for success. But if you want people to succeed, you have to be willing to teach them. So we have formalized a teaching culture. We teach and coach every day."

To be honest, my going-in assumption was that Pal's rigorous screening of its applicants, the hours and hours of training it requires, and its never-ending commitment to certification and recertification would make for a workforce that is uptight, stressed-out, anxious about screwing up and suffering the consequences. In fact, just the opposite is true. When I spent time behind the counter, in the kitchen, and in the storage rooms, I was struck by how calm, methodical, and even-keeled the atmosphere was—the opposite of Lucy and Ethel on the chocolate-candy assembly line. The system is so carefully designed, and everyone in the restaurant so well trained, that the operation can be fast without being furious, relentless without being joyless.

The result of this culture is that employees at Pal's show the same sense of loyalty as its customers. Turnover numbers are absurdly low. In thirty-three years of operation, only seven general managers (the people who run individual locations) have left the company voluntarily. Seven! Annual turnover among assistant managers is 1.4 percent, vanishingly low for a field where people jump from company to company and often exit the industry altogether. Even among frontline employees, the part-timers and high schoolers who can be so tough for most organizations to rely on, turnover is one third the industry average. "People ask me, 'What if you spend all this time and money on training and someone leaves?'" Crosby says. "I ask them, 'What if we don't spend the time and money, and they stay?'"

Crosby takes his teaching responsibilities seriously—and personally. For example, Pal's has assembled a master reading list for all the leaders in the company, twenty-one books that range from timeless classics by Machiavelli (*The Prince*), Sun Tzu (*The Art of War*), Dale Carnegie (*How to Win Friends and Influence People*), and Max De Pree (*Leadership Is an Art*) to highly technical tomes on quality, lean management, and day-to-day execution. Crosby runs a book club to delve into the material. Every other Monday, he invites five managers from different locations to discuss one of the books on the master list. "All five of them have to read the book and give a presentation," he says. "'Here's what I learned, here's how it applies to Pal's, here's what I am committing to change, here's how I am helping people in my operation grasp the concepts and put them to work.'"

Meanwhile, every day, he identifies at least one subject he will teach to one person in the company. Actually, that's a requirement for all leaders at Pal's, who are expected to spend 10 percent of their time on teaching, and to identify a target subject and a target student every day. On the day I visited, Crosby had three teaching sessions on his schedule. The first was about personal productivity: "When is a job really done? You spend time on something, you 'finish' it, but the fringes are not wrapped up tight. So is it done?" The second was about the creative side of the business: "I talked with someone about what we call the 'chef's mentality.' We spend lots of time on process. But we are in the food business, so we have to think like chefs." The third was a classic management topic, working with a store leader on the sales-forecasting system. "You need to make these formal teaching commitments," Crosby says. "If you teach valuable subjects to the right people, you move the needle as a brand and as a business."

This teaching mentality is so ingrained in the Pal's culture that it has become the primary regulator of the company's growth strategy—which, for all its success and acclaim, is much more modest than it could be. Over the last ten years or so, quick-serve joints with a sense of style (think In-N-Out Burger on the West

Coast or Danny Meyer's Shake Shack on the East Coast) have exploded into the public consciousness and become a mouthwatering destination for investors. (Shake Shack's IPO in January 2015 valued the sixty-three-restaurant company at more than $1 billion.) Given that Pal's is so wildly popular among its customers, and such an icon in its region, it could be racing to add new locations, even new parts of the country, much faster than it has. So why, I asked CEO Thom Crosby, has the company been so restrained in its growth trajectory?

"We could grow faster, and there will be some acceleration as we get bigger," he replied. "But we are very conservative. The thing to us about size, where we see so many others get it wrong, is that they believe growth is about real estate and financial resources. Growth for us is about people and leadership development. Our concept is, let's develop a leader until they push us to a point where we say, 'We can't *not* build a store for you, because you're such a superstar.' Growth is not just about markets or demographics. It's people ahead of everything else."

Even as Crosby and his colleagues are fanatical about the teaching mentality inside Pal's, it informs their relationship with the outside world as well. Over time, as the company's management prowess became the stuff of legend in certain business circles, especially after the Baldrige Award, more and more executives asked to see for themselves what the fuss was about. So Pal's decided to create an institution to teach other companies to do what it has done—not how to make a Big Chicken or a Toasted Cheese, but how to strive for extraordinary in a world with far too much ordinary. Every month, sometimes twice a month, the Pal's Business Excellence Institute convenes a two-day master class in

Kingsport on the ideas, systems, metrics, and techniques behind the company's enormous success. These classes, which sell out weeks in advance, attract students from a diverse set of fields and professional backgrounds.

The session I attended included visitors from hospitality companies, manufacturers, the construction business, a ballet troupe, a public-school system, and, of course, several quick-serve outfits. For many of the organizations in the room, this was the second, third, even fourth time they'd sent staff members to study the Pal's business model. Like the company's restaurants, the Pal's Business Excellence Institute "is kind of a cult," one attendee joked to me. And if not a cult, at least a learning laboratory that inspires lots of enthusiasm and passion. K&N Management, based in Austin, Texas, and the second restaurant outfit ever to win the Baldrige, visited Pal's *fourteen times* over nine years to learn the secrets of its success.

Why do these companies bother to flock to Kingsport? What makes Pal's tick? How do the company's leaders and rank-and-file employees maintain the passion to keep pursuing perfection even in a field as imperfect as fast food? The more I listened to the instructors and watched my fellow students, the more I came to appreciate the missionary mind-set, the shared passions among teachers and students to feel like they were building something special, that they were thinking bigger and aiming higher than others in their field. David McClaskey, cofounder and president of the institute, began the two-day session with a message that was directly relevant to everyone in the class—and to everyone reading this book.

"I have a lot of respect for average," he told the group. "In most industries, it is not easy to be average. But we choose to be extraordinary. And it *is* a choice. The world will not demand it of you. You have to fight for it. Every day, people have to ask themselves, 'What am I willing to do that the ordinary leader is not willing to do?' The world will not force you to be extraordinary. You must demand it of yourselves."

> **"In most industries, it is not easy to be average. But we choose to be extraordinary. And it *is* a choice. The world will not demand it of you."**

"NOTHING CLARIFIES LIKE CLARITY" —WHY THE BEST LEADERS TALK THE WALK

One of the most ubiquitous aphorisms in organizational life is that the best leaders "walk the talk." They understand that their behavior and day-to-day actions have to match the aspirations they have for their colleagues and the operation as a whole. But the more time I spend with market-making innovators and high-performing companies, the more I appreciate that leaders also have to "talk the walk." They must be able to explain, in language that is unique to their field and compelling to their colleagues and customers, why what they do matters and how they expect to win. Ultimately, as I've tried to demonstrate in these first two chapters, the only sustainable form of business leadership is thought leadership. Which is why leaders who *think* differently about their business invariably *talk* about it differently as well.

Vernon Hill is so obsessed with the role of language at Metro Bank that when he published a book in Great Britain about his personal story and business lessons, he included a glossary of forty-one words and phrases that have special importance at the bank and help to create a shared understanding at every level about what makes Metro tick. Pal's Sudden Service doesn't just have its own vocabulary, it has its own *curriculum*—courseware, reading lists, and lesson plans that distill into rich language the ideas that drive the company forward and distinguish it from more mundane players in its field. Liisa Joronen and her colleagues in Helsinki have such a granular way of explaining what they call the SOL Operating System that it becomes easy to understand their one-of-a-kind ideas, even if they are hard to replicate by outsiders who don't share the company's point of view about elevating the roles and responsibilities of frontline workers.

Still, I'm not sure I've ever seen the power of language come so vividly to life as I did when I participated in a daylong orientation held roughly every six weeks for new "team members" of Quicken Loans, the online mortgage lender based in Detroit and founded by high-profile billionaire Dan Gilbert, the fiery owner of the Cleveland Cavaliers and the business leader most associated with the Motor City's economic-comeback strategy. Like Gilbert himself, Quicken Loans is famous for lots of things, from torrid growth (the company closed a record $200 billion worth of mortgage volume since 2013, making it the second-largest mortgage lender in the United States, ahead of Bank of America) to much-praised customer service (it is a perennial J.D. Power customer-satisfaction winner) to its intense and outgoing corporate culture, which ranks it high every year among *Fortune*'s "100 Best Companies to Work

For" and "*Computerworld*'s Best Places to Work in IT." But behind all the growth and success, at the heart of the company's approach to strategy, service, and culture, is a language system that defines life inside the organization and captures the missionary zeal behind its success. You can't understand why Quicken wins unless you understand how it talks.[7]

Founder Dan Gilbert and CEO Bill Emerson call this language the company's "ISMs," which is why the rollicking, fast-paced, eight-hour orientation session is called "ISMs in Action." ISMs are short, pithy statements of philosophy, values, and behavior that capture the essence of life at Quicken Loans. "Numbers and money follow, they do not lead." "Innovation is rewarded, execution is worshipped." "Simplicity is genius." "Every second counts." "We are the 'they.'"

Gilbert and Emerson, who present separately and together over the entire eight hours an executive teaching marathon unlike anything I have witnessed, march team members through the ISMs with slide shows, stand-up humor, war stories, and unabashed appeals to the heart. A few of the ISMs get covered in ten or fifteen minutes, some take as much as an hour, even more. But the result is a full-day immersion in a whole new language—a vocabulary of competition that helps to set the company apart in the marketplace and hold its people together in the workplace. It's also an opportunity to watch how frenetic, hard-charging, supremely confident business executives flat-out enjoy the power of words to shape minds and guide action. "Things that are easy to do in the beginning are usually hard to live with in the end," Bill Emerson warned early in his presentation. "If you weren't you, would you do business with you?" asked Dan Gilbert, perhaps channeling the wisdom and spirit of Yogi Berra.

Interestingly, several of the attendees with whom I spoke weren't even new to the company. They'd come back to ISMs Day for a refresher course, a reminder, an opportunity to reacquaint themselves with the language that defines life at Quicken Loans, a chance to spend a day watching the founder and the CEO talk the walk. "This is not about what we do, it's about who we are," Dan Gilbert told the audience. "When you know who you are, then all of the decisions you have to make become a lot easier. When decisions are easier to make, things get better faster. Nothing clarifies like clarity."

On the day I attended, more than a thousand participants crowded into a ballroom in the Marriott at the Renaissance Center on the banks of the Detroit River to immerse themselves in the company's nineteen ISMs and the worldview they are meant to capture. Oddly, the first thing I noticed were rubber wristbands for attendees with the inscription "You'll see it when you believe it," an echo (no doubt unintentional) of Ralph Hodgson's memorable turn of phrase. (It's ISM number 11, actually.) After some loud music and an audience-wide wave, Gilbert and Emerson got down to business. They urged their colleagues to embrace the belief that "The inches we need are everywhere around us"—in other words, there are countless small opportunities for people to tweak a product, improve a process, reduce a cost, that lead to big wins. (That's the second of the company's nineteen ISMs.) They insisted, no excuses allowed, that everyone agree with the ISM "Responding with a sense of urgency is the ante to play." Gilbert personally emphasized again and again, sometimes with jokes, sometimes with withering disdain, the absolute requirement that Quicken employees return every phone call and every e-mail on the same business day they are received. "We are zealots about this," he thundered, "we are on the lunatic fringe" (the same language, interestingly enough, used by Vernon Hill and the bankers at Metro). "And if you're 'too busy' to do it, I'll do it for you"—at which point he gave out his direct-dial extension and promised to return calls for any of his overwhelmed colleagues.

On and on it went—funny stories, sage pieces of advice, a rapid-fire history of the company that underscored the ideas and insights behind its rise to prominence. But mainly an iteration and reiteration of the company's nineteen ISMs. What's more, everything about the day, from the look and feel of the vast ballroom to the smallest details of how the company's leaders presented their material, was meant to bring those ISMs to life. More than once I was struck by how CEO Bill Emerson, a member of Penn State's 1982 national championship football team, almost physically became the ISM he was explaining. During a long (and oddly memorable) explanation of the power of body language in human interactions, its importance even when people are communicating over the phone rather than face-to-face, he was literally lying flat on the stage, trying to under-score the shortcomings of a passive approach to important conversations. "You cannot create enthusiasm sitting on your butt!" he thundered. "You have to be engaged, you have to move around!"

Leaders who *think* differently about their business invariably *talk* about it differently as well.

What was even more striking than what I saw during "ISMs in Action" was what I saw after I left the session and spent time in different corners of the company trying to understand how leadership's obsession with language manifested itself in the day-to-day realities of life inside the company. Those connections were not hard to find. The commitment to sustained, small-bore innovations (one of its ISMs is to be "obsessed with finding a better way") means that Gilbert and Emerson love to talk about the virtues of "building a better mousetrap" in every element of how the business operates. So the company has a Mousetrap Department, created more than ten years ago, whose members (called Mousetrappers) search for small ways to make things smarter, faster, cheaper, more consistent. Meanwhile, the Cheese Factory (get it?) solicits ideas from across the company on every nook and cranny of how the business can be improved, vets the ideas, and then helps get them implemented. In a typical year, the Cheese Factory receives more than 7,000 ideas and implements more than 1,000 of them.

Among the company's 1,200 IT professionals, the signature program for rapid-fire innovation is what's called Bullet Time (a different metaphor that would require too long an explanation). Every Monday afternoon for four hours, members of the IT staff, alone or in teams, work on projects of their own choosing, at their own pace, as long as those projects represent a clear break from what they normally do. (The projects do not have to offer direct benefits to the company.) "Innovation is no longer about people in lab coats tucked away for six months or a year, emerging from some secret place with a 'disruptive' technology," explains Bill Parker, a senior IT leader and the person most responsible for starting Bullet Time back in 2011. "If you make lightning strike a thousand times, you're going to start fires all over the place. That's the logic of how things evolve and improve."

Ultimately, though, the most persuasive example of the power of language inside Quicken Loans, the direct connection between how its leaders talk and how the organization performs, is the way the company recruits and trains its mortgage bankers. These are the people who drive the top line of the business, the revenue generators who field calls from prospective clients, size up their creditworthiness, help them organize their personal finances, determine their goals, complete the government-required forms, and get the loan—all over the Internet or by telephone. It's a fast-paced, detail-oriented, emotionally fraught kind of job, in which the typical mortgage banker has more than a thousand monthly interactions with clients—which means a thousand opportunities not to live up to the standards of focus, service, and immediate response that the ISMs reinforce.

Which is why, explains Michelle Salvatore, who spent more than a decade as a senior recruiting executive at Quicken Loans, only 20 percent of the mortgage bankers the company hires come with a banking background. (The fast-growing organization, which has more than 1,000 job openings at any time, employs some 130 people to find, interview, evaluate, and do background checks on recruits.) It hires more than 125 mortgage bankers per month in Detroit alone, along with bankers based in satellite locations in Ohio, Arizona, and North Carolina. "We don't really like our bankers to have prior industry experience," she says, "because we have to retrain them away from what they learned elsewhere."

Tony Nuckolls, vice president of training and leadership development, who joined the company back in 1996 and was a founding member of the Mortgage-in-a-Box team, the innovation that gave rise to the modern Quicken Loans, underscores Salvatore's point.

"If we can bring someone in as a blank canvas, we can train them up, immerse them in our ways of thinking, our ways of behaving, our ways of treating clients," says Nuckolls, who is something of a legend inside the company. "We've had people come to us from the industry and it's really hard to break some of their habits."

The signature experience for new bankers, called, in classic Quicken Loans style, Banker Greatness Training, is in part a deep dive into the technical process from beginning to end—the laws, regulations, software systems, credit factors, and financial analytics required to be a highly skilled (and government-licensed) mortgage professional in any environment. But the heart of the experience, which lasts as long as six months, is all about human behaviors that trace directly to the ISMs championed by Dan Gilbert and Bill Emerson—service, energy, decision making, problem solving, and communication to be a high performer in the Quicken Loans environment.

"We practice like crazy," Tony Nuckolls explains, "we practice more than anyone else in this space. We listen to phone calls with clients, we break down those calls and analyze how our bankers are behaving. We look at these calls the way an NBA team looks at game film: 'This is what a good call sounds like, this is what it looks like, this is an interaction that brings our brand promise to life, this is a call that didn't live up to our standards.' Great mortgage bankers at this place are phenomenal listeners, they know how to assess the real goals of their clients, they have a sense of urgency, they want things done yesterday. If we're doing our job right, and they are the right people for the job at Quicken Loans, they understand that being a mortgage banker here is new, unique, different, and they like it."

PART II

Don't Let What You Know Limit What You Can Imagine

Expertise is powerful . . . until it gets in the way of innovation. In a world being remade before our eyes, leaders who make a big difference are the ones who challenge the logic of their field—and of their own success.

Chapter 3

BEYOND THE PARADOX OF EXPERTISE

"Too Often, Pride in Your Most Recent Idea Becomes a Barrier to Seeing the Next Idea"

I t's 4:20 A.M., more than an hour before sunrise on a cold, windy, miserable May morning in New Haven, Connecticut. I'd like to be back at the hotel—out of the elements, snug in bed. Instead, I am strolling the New Haven Green, struck by the wealth and history that surrounds me. Three picture-postcard centuries-old churches attest to the religious origins of this spot, which was built in 1638 by the city's founders and designed to be spacious enough to accommodate those who would be spared at the Second Coming. Just off the green, Phelps Gate marks the entrance to the Old Campus of Yale University, and bears the school's lofty motto *Lux et veritas* (Light and truth). Nearby, the Colonial-era Nicholas Callahan House serves as home to one of the oldest of Yale's so-called secret societies, those bastions of wealth and privilege that remain a mysterious part of life at the elite school. The white-clapboard structure is off-limits to anyone who is not a member. (So much for light and truth.)

I am not walking the green to revel in its high-minded Puritan past, or to get an early start on the high-achieving undergraduates sound asleep in their nearby dorms. I am here, in the spirit of that Garth Brooks song, to make friends in low places—to find, meet, and spend a few minutes with members of the chronically home-less population in downtown New Haven. Some of them are easy to spot, resting on a bench or killing time on church steps. Others are more elusive, tucked away in an alley, curled up in a restaurant doorway. Wherever they may be, there are more than first meet the eye. Indeed, as darkness loses its grip on the green, as the sun be-gins to rise, homeless people emerge seemingly from nowhere to begin another day—their silent, lonely, largely invisible version of the morning rush hour.

The point of this visit, why I am here, along with 180 volunteers who have fanned out in small teams across Greater New Haven, is to shine a light, literally and figuratively, on this overlooked popu-lation. These high-energy canvassers, drawn from the ranks of so-cial workers, church groups, college students, and United Way volunteers, will go out in the predawn hours for three straight mornings as part of an initiative called the 100-Day Challenge. Lo-cal housing advocates estimate that 120 or so chronically homeless people survive on the streets in and around New Haven. (The total homeless population is much larger, of course, but most of them are on the street for days, weeks, or a few months before they find a place to live, unlike the chronically homeless, who have been on the street for at least a year, and often much longer.)

The first step in this challenge is to identify people who have struggled for a long period of time, take their photos, record their personal and medical histories, and analyze who among them is at greatest risk for violence, disease, or death. Some are eager to share their stories, others less so, but even the reluctant ones open up once they're offered a McDonald's gift card. Calmly, compassionately, and quickly (fewer than ten minutes), our team asks a series of questions that will be used to establish a Vulnerability Index for each person: "How long have you been on the street or in shelters?" "In the past six months, how many times have you been taken to the hospital in an ambulance?" "Does anybody force or trick you to do things you don't want to do?" "Do you have planned activities each day other than just surviving that bring you happiness and fulfillment?"

Once the canvass is complete and the data analyzed, the next step is to move urgently and nimbly to find housing for the most vulnerable members of this painfully vulnerable population. Not to grab them a spot at a shelter for a week, or to bring them in from the cold for a night, but to place them in houses or apartments that will be their permanent homes—whether they're clean and sober (often a prerequisite for housing assistance), whether they have insights into their mental-health issues (another standard condition). In other words, not to manage the problems of these people, or to judge who is most worthy of help, but to end chronic homelessness once and for all among those most at risk of dying on the streets.

What's so impressive about this hard-charging initiative is that its goals were as tangible as they were ambitious: to find permanent places to live for 75 percent of the city's chronically homeless population by July 30, precisely one hundred days after the challenge was announced. What's even more impressive is that what's happening in New Haven is one piece of a movement across the country to craft dramatically new ways to eliminate chronic homelessness—a movement that has made big waves even as it has had a huge impact, and that has overturned some of the most deep-seated assumptions of the most experienced leaders in the field.

The 100,000 Homes Campaign was unveiled in July 2010 by an organization based in New York City called Community Solutions. The "moon shot" goal was to provide permanent housing for 100,000 chronically homeless Americans within four years without a huge boost in government resources (there was little hope of that), without scripting in advance how the goal would be reached (organizers trumpeted the virtues of improvisation and adaptation), but with no room for doubt that it would be reached. The initiative was organized around a manifesto that spelled out its defining principles and described an entirely new model for addressing a painfully intractable problem. "The time has come," the manifesto declared, "to stop managing homelessness and start ending it."

One of the manifesto's core principles was Housing First: "The only lasting solution to homelessness is permanent housing. Far too often, however, we treat the symptoms of homelessness instead of its root cause." Another was Know Who's Out There: "We cannot end homelessness in America until every homeless person on our streets is known by name by someone who has carefully assessed their health and housing needs." A third principle was Track Your Progress: "We cannot end homelessness until every community rigorously tracks and measures its progress on a monthly basis and makes calculated adjustments to improve performance."

Ultimately, 186 cities and towns embraced the core principles of the manifesto and designed grassroots efforts to find permanent housing for their chronically homeless populations. As the campaign unfolded, local activists, equipped and connected by Community Solutions, shared what they tried, reported on what worked poorly or well, and suggested how other places could improve on the techniques with which they had experimented. On July 30, 2014, just as New Haven was tallying the final numbers for its 100-Day Challenge (housing 102 people), the 100,000 Homes Campaign announced its nationwide results—permanent housing for 105,580 chronically homeless people, one of the most dramatic, tangible, game-changing advances in the history of the field. To be sure, the overall problem of homelessness remains stubbornly persistent, rising and falling with the state of the economy, investments in mental health, and all sorts of other socioeconomic factors. But in the case of chronic homelessness, those who have been without shelter for a year or more, the progress is palpable.

"Is there anything more thrilling, more satisfying, than solving a big, important problem?" asks Rosanne Haggerty, founder and president of Community Solutions, the innovator most responsible for the 100,000 Homes Campaign. "But in my field, social services, people who spend their lives managing problems almost never have the satisfaction of solving them. Nobody I know signed up to work on homelessness for job security. But somehow we created a 'homeless-industrial complex' that is good at running programs, but has given up on solving the problem. We realized that doing more of the same was absurd. We asked organizations to wrestle with the consequences of doing business differently."

In many ways, Rosanne Haggerty is an unlikely candidate to issue such an edgy challenge to conventional wisdom in her field. She is one of the country's most recognized, influential, and dauntless advocates for the homeless—a certified member of the social-services establishment. Over the past twenty-five years, her work has been chronicled in the media, has been funded by high-powered backers from J.P.Morgan to Ben & Jerry's, and won her a MacArthur "genius grant." Back in 1990, she founded an organization called Common Ground that earned support and acclaim for its strategy of acquiring run-down properties in New York City and turning them into well-designed, highly functional facilities to serve the homeless. Her first such project, a $36 million renovation of the 652-unit Times Square Hotel, opened to great fanfare in 1993. Next, in 1999, came the 416-room Prince George Hotel, once a landmark property that had fallen into disrepair and was reno-vated (price tag: $40 million) to provide housing for low-income adults, the chronically homeless, and people living with HIV/AIDS. And on it went, from The Andrews in the Bowery (price tag: $14 million) to The Brook in the Bronx (price tag: $43 million).

"Most homeless shelters don't have ballrooms," declared the *Wall Street Journal* in an in-depth profile of Haggerty's work and the properties Common Ground had renovated or built. "Walking into the elegant lobby of New York's old Prince George Hotel, with its richly hued woodwork, feels like you've entered some Merchant Ivory movie, not a residence for displaced persons." The *Journal* marveled at the property's "benign and inclusive form of gentrifica-tion," and went back to describing the ballroom, with its "restored coffered ceilings by gilded-age architect Howard Greenley."

All told, between 1990 and 2011, Common Ground renovated or built three thousand units to serve the homeless population in New York City and a few other locations—a remarkable achievement by any measure. But the more buildings Common Ground opened, the more dissatisfied Haggerty became. For one thing, the strategy for which Common Ground had become famous required huge amounts of time and even bigger piles of money. Worse, as she looked out on Times Square, she realized that some of the most vulnerable people on the streets, those most in need of what she had created, either weren't interested in her properties or weren't qualified to live there based on the eligibility criteria the facilities had established for their residents. "It was like we had built a hospital," Haggerty says, "and decided to exclude the sickest people in the city."[1]

So she gave herself a new challenge, and launched an experiment to figure out how to meet it. What if she and her colleagues looked beyond the properties they were renovating and building and focused instead on the flesh-and-blood population they were serving? Specifically, what if they set a wildly ambitious target—to reduce chronic homelessness in Times Square by two thirds within three years—and did whatever it took to hit that target? How could they identify the chronically homeless, as opposed to those who had stumbled briefly onto hard times? What conditions would they impose (or refrain from imposing) on those they were helping? What new allies would they need to enlist to find housing fast rather than build it themselves? What kinds of leadership skills would be required to run this experiment?

This last question might have been the most important. As her Street-to-Home initiative began to take shape, Haggerty recruited a leader with no background in social services, advocacy for the homeless, or real-estate development—and thus none of the baggage of lifers in the field. Becky Margiotta, a West Point graduate, had spent nine years as an army officer, much of it as a captain in special-operations settings, before she was brought to Haggerty's attention by one of her professors at the academy. From the outset, she attacked homelessness in Times Square with a military-style sense of urgency, an appreciation for "boots-on-the-ground intelligence," and a willingness to improvise under difficult conditions without compromising the timeline or the goal. "My military training has shaped my thinking on just about everything," she says. "Missions first, troops always. Do whatever it takes to get the job done, and take care of your people."

Indeed, some of the techniques she devised to get the job done traced back to tactics developed by the U.S. military. One of the defining features of the Times Square project, for example, was the push to interview and photograph the local homeless population. It was vital to get to know each person's story, Haggerty and Margiotta realized, figure out who was at greatest risk of disease or death, and put actual names to faces. (Hence the manifesto's principle Know Who's Out There.) But how? Then the former army captain thought about the house-to-house, village-by-village push early in the U.S. invasion of Iraq to find members of Saddam Hussein's inner circle who had gone underground. Might that same sensibility inform their push to find the chronically homeless?

"Remember how U.S. troops got playing cards with faces of the most-wanted bad guys on them?" Margiotta asks. "We didn't create playing cards, and we weren't looking for bad guys, but we needed a way to figure out who had been homeless for months or years versus who was passing through on Wednesdays because they serve macaroni and cheese at the soup kitchen, who was reasonably healthy versus who was dying from stage-four liver cancer." That intense focus on individuals and their stories generated some intense pushback from old pros in the field.

"The status-quo social workers were up in arms," Margiotta

says. "How disrespectful! What about privacy and human dignity? But we took photos only when we got permission. And when you make this work person-specific, when you put faces to names, it makes the folks who want to keep things the way they are, whether they mean to or not, very uncomfortable. And if you're making folks uncomfortable, you're doing something right."

What happened in Times Square over the next three years set the stage, intellectually and organizationally, for what I saw unfold on the New Haven Green and what happened across the country during the 100,000 Homes Campaign. The results of the experiment were so compelling that Haggerty decided to leave Common Ground, start Community Solutions, and launch the nationwide movement—with Becky Margiotta as director.

"Our goals for Times Square seemed impossible when we set them," Haggerty says, "but they forced us to disrupt our old ways of thinking. Too often, pride in your most recent idea becomes a barrier to seeing the next idea. I was trapped in my own 'housing bubble.' We had to ask, 'What better idea do we have?' This was our better idea."

"DON'T BE AFRAID TO CHANGE YOUR PERSPECTIVE" —THE POWER OF PROVOCATIVE COMPETENCE

Expertise is powerful—until it gets in the way of innovation. One of the sobering lessons of the great transformations in business, leadership, and society in the last few decades is that the people and organizations with the most experience, knowledge, and resources in a particular field are often the last ones to see and seize opportunities for something dramatically new. It's basically the inverse of the phenomenon we described in chapter 1, when organizations and leaders lose their appetite for taking risks because they worry about a competitive backlash from incumbents who realize (usually far too late, it turns out) that a new idea is taking hold in the market.

But where were those slow-to-respond established giants, overflowing with smart people and big budgets, in the first place? Why couldn't ABC, CBS, or some other media powerhouse launch the first twenty-four-hour news network, rather than leave it to Ted Turner, a novice in the communications business who inherited his father's billboard company? Why didn't one of the global music labels migrate its artists onto the nascent platform of cable television, rather than allow Robert Pittman, a twentysomething radio programmer, to create MTV and reshape the pop-culture landscape? Why was General Motors so late to embrace the allure of hybrid cars, Microsoft so slow to recognize the rise of the Internet (even though it wiped out Netscape), Yahoo! so clueless about the promise and outrageous economic value of Google and/or Facebook, both of which it had opportunities to buy in their early days as private companies?

The story line has become so familiar that the questions almost answer themselves: All too often, what we know limits what we can imagine. Cynthia Barton Rabe, a former innovation strategist at Intel, coined a memorable term to describe this debilitating form of strategic blindness. Too many companies and leaders, often the best companies and the most successful leaders, struggle with what she calls the "paradox of expertise"—the frustrating reality that the more deeply immersed you are in a market, a product category, or a technology, the harder it becomes to open your mind to new business models that may reshape that market or promising ways to leapfrog that technology. Past results may not be the enemy of subsequent breakthroughs, but they can constrain the capacity to grasp the future.

"When it comes to innovation," she argues, "the same hard-won experience, best practices, and processes that are the cornerstones of an organization's success may be more like millstones that threaten to sink it. Said another way, the weight of what we know, especially what we collectively 'know,' kills innovation. . . . Why can knowledge and experience be so lethal to innovation? Because when we become expert, we often trade our 'what if' flights of fancy for the grounded reality of 'what is.'"[2]

People with the most experience are often the last ones to see and seize opportunities for something dramatically new.

In other words, the more closely you've looked at a field, and the longer you've been looking at it in the same way, the more difficult it can be to see new patterns, prospects, or possibilities. Amy E. Herman, a consultant and educator trained as a lawyer and an art historian, has created an intriguing program that gets to the heart of the all-important difference between looking and seeing. In the Art of Perception, she takes police detectives, FBI agents, even officials from the Secret Service and the CIA, to the Metropolitan Museum of Art, the Frick Collection, and other well-known galleries.

These grizzled observers of crime and terrorism, trained to look in certain ways for clues about solving murders or identifying threats, instead set their sights on works from Picasso, Caravaggio, Edward Hopper, and other masters. The exercise is "not about looking at art," Herman explains to the participants, "it's about talking about what you see."[3]

Or, much of the time, what you *don't* see. Time after time, skilled observers miss critical elements of a painting that send an important message, overlook signposts in a scene that speak to what's taking place, or simply can't figure out how to describe what's right in front of them. (Participants are not allowed to use the words *obviously* and *clearly*, nor can they point at the art to describe a feature or a scene. Instead, they are required to express their insights verbally to their colleagues.) "Don't be afraid to change your perspective," she urges her students, who report that the new ways of seeing that they develop through these art-museum visits have opened their eyes to new ways of evaluating evidence on the job.

Amy Herman's seminar is an elegant departure from the everyday routines of life as a police detective or a CIA agent, a fun and clever intervention that sharpens skills and clears heads. "In New York, the extraordinary is ordinary to us, so in training we're always looking to become even more aware as observers," a deputy chief explained in one of many approving accounts of the program. But is there a more sustained way to transcend the paradox of expertise, a mind-set that draws on the best of what's come before without closing off what may come next? If there is, and the history of big change in long-established organizations suggests it's not easy, it involves a style of engaging with the world best captured by the term "provocative competence."

I first encountered the notion of provocative competence from the marketers at FCB (Foote, Cone & Belding), one of the world's oldest ad agencies. (In recent years, FCB has done high-profile, award-winning work for clients such as Levi's, Kmart, and HP, among many others.) I'd been invited to speak at a meeting at FCB's Chicago offices, the largest in its global network, but quickly decided to say less and listen more. The executives and planners there had developed an approach to the business, complete with handbooks and workbooks, organized around what they called "calculated boldness"—brand ideas that were "simple, relevant, and persuasive," but also "scary, challenging, and abruptive." To arrive at these ideas, they held what they called Strategic Rumbles—all-day sessions to interrogate the history of a product and generate edgy, original insights into the future. ("Find the investigative equivalent of hanging upside down, dressing incognito, or standing on a chair," one handbook says.)

Ultimately, though, for any of these techniques to matter, creative types and account managers alike had to be what the agency called provocatively competent. What did that mean, exactly? It meant "consciously junking structure to let new order emerge in a very conscious way," turning away from "your own ingrained habits and the forms and formulae that have been forced upon you." It's not enough "just to be competent," FCB's leaders explained, "that just enables average work that fails to inspire." Nor is it enough "to just be provocative—that's where creativity forgets its purpose and serves itself more than the business." Rather than fight those two impulses, they counseled their colleagues to "embrace the duality. Be firmly competent—thorough, smart, business-minded, accountable. And boundlessly provocative—challenging, surprising,

restless, imaginative." And they urged them to "practice provocative competence in everything we do. Every assignment we frame,
every brief we write, every idea we float, every conversation we
have."[4]

As it turns out, the term *provocative competence* was not coined
by a bunch of marketing wizards in Chicago. It goes back to the
world of jazz, and captures how the most adventuresome musicians
transcend their well-honed mastery to open space for improvisation. The best bandleaders, like the best business leaders, "create
the discrepancy and dissonance that trigger people to move away
from habitual positions and repetitive patterns," argues Frank
J. Barrett, professor of management at the Naval Postgraduate
School and an accomplished musician himself. (He has led his own
bands and toured with the Tommy Dorsey Orchestra.) It was Barrett who first used the term, years ago, to describe how giants like
Duke Ellington and Miles Davis would commit to "stretching themselves to play in challenging contexts."

**"Be firmly competent—thorough, smart,
business-minded, accountable. And boundlessly
provocative—challenging, surprising, restless,
imaginative."**

In his captivating book *Yes to the Mess*, Barrett draws all sorts
of leadership lessons from jazz, none more relevant than the power
of provocative competence. So-so musicians, he says, allow themselves to fall into the "competency trap"—they rely on "licks that

have been greeted enthusiastically in past performances, to become in effect imitations of themselves." Great musicians manage
to "outwit their learned habits by putting themselves in unfamiliar
musical situations demanding novel responses." Ultimately, Barrett explains, provocative competence is "leadership that enlivens
activity and rouses the mind to life."[5]

Provocative competence is more than a metaphor. According
to Barrett, it is a methodology, a process for bandleaders and business leaders to make sure that what they know doesn't limit what
they can imagine. It begins with an "affirmative move"—encouraging
colleagues to do something they might not otherwise do, "seeing
other people's strengths better than they see their own strengths."
The next step involves "introducing a small disruption to routine"—
something that "engages people to be mindful, to pay attention in
new ways." It's also important to "create situations that demand
activity"—to persuade people to "try and try again, to keep trying
and discovering as they go." Leaders facilitate learning by "encouraging repetition"—creating "moments of gradual insight and slowly
evaporating safety." Finally, provocative competence requires an
"analogic sharpening of perspectives"—room for people to "jump
into the morass as they make comparisons, links, and connections
to a larger emerging whole."

"NOTHING WE DO HERE IS WHAT YOU EXPECT" —LEADING OUTSIDE THE LINES (LITERALLY)

For an eye-opening case study on the power of provocative competence, a leadership outlook that "enlivens activity and rouses the

mind to life," look no further than the rise to prominence, as a business and as a cultural landmark, of a parking garage in Miami
Beach, Florida. That's right, a parking garage. The seven-story structure sits at the corner of Lincoln and Alton roads, the entrance to a
world-famous pedestrian thoroughfare that attracts visitors from
around the world. The structure, known as 1111 Lincoln Road,
serves about as mundane a function as can be imagined—it's a
place to park cars (roughly three hundred in total) as their owners
stroll the shops of Miami Beach and walk the sands of South Beach.
Yet nothing about the facility is mundane. When real-estate developer Robert Wennett acquired the space in 2005, it was a homely
parking lot situated alongside a bland office building designed in
the Brutalist style. He vowed to turn something blandly functional
into something genuinely remarkable—not because he wanted to
"innovate," but because he wanted to reinterpret the original vision
of Lincoln Road, set back in 1910 by Carl G. Fisher, the legendary
father of Miami Beach, for a new era of culture and commerce.

"We wanted to connect back to the founding purpose of Lincoln Road at the spot that was the original entrance to Lincoln
Road," says Wennett, who had a long, successful history in commercial real estate before he took on this game-changing, career-
defining project. Wennett spent two decades as a top executive
with major real-estate investment companies, where he oversaw
portfolios worth billions of dollars and developed a reputation as
someone who appreciated the importance of community as well as
commerce. Yet nothing in his portfolio was as arresting, or as original, as what took shape in Miami Beach.

The new facility opened in spring 2010 to widespread critical
acclaim and loud popular applause. One reporter celebrated the

building as a unique work of "carchitecture," which he defined as "the unimaginable marriage of high-end architecture and car storage." This was how he described his initial reaction to the place: "Parking garages, the grim afterthought of American design, call to mind many words. (Rats. Beer cans. Unidentifiable smells.) Breathtaking is not usually among them."

But this parking garage is breathtaking, so much so that it has become an in-demand venue not just for motorists but for charity functions, wine tastings, and celebrity gatherings. "This is not a parking garage," Wennett has said. "It's really a civic space." Indeed, the top floor was designed to hold both cars and events, and there have been some doozies over the years. LeBron James, in his final season as a member of the Miami Heat, hosted a wild celebration there for his eleventh Nike shoe. Where better to have the LeBron James "11/11 Experience" than at 1111 Lincoln Road? One year later, during Art Basel Miami, *Paper* magazine marked its infamous cover shoot of Kim Kardashian (featuring her larger-than-life posterior) with a "Break the Internet" bash on the seventh floor of the garage.

Today, the facility is its own high-profile brand ("Meet me at eleven eleven," residents routinely say), with an instantly recognizable logo and universal name recognition in Miami Beach. It can be decidedly more expensive to park here than in more mundane locations (hourly rates run as much as four times higher than those charged by other lots) and the price tags in many of the complex's shops are not for the faint of heart. But 1111 Lincoln Road stands out as a compelling destination, and a prosperous business, precisely because it stands as an alternative to conventional wisdom and expectations.

"Everything we do in the garage is not what you expect in a parking garage," Robert Wennett told a video producer who made a short film about the creation of 1111. "We said to ourselves, 'Let's look at what a parking garage is, and then let's twist every single notion about it.'" Wennett, it should be noted, doesn't just talk the talk. He *lives* the talk. He built his home on the top floor of the structure, in a penthouse apartment with views that are even more spectacular than the design of the garage. "People always ask me, 'Why would you choose to live in a parking garage?'" he cracks. "But the moment they walk in, they never ask again."[6]

After hearing about Wennett's work from senior executives in the luxury field, and watching a video about what he'd built, I had no choice but to travel to South Beach, see it for myself, and spend time with the person who created it. The place lived up to the hype. The $65 million structure features exaggerated ceilings, wide-open 360-degree views, no exterior walls—more like a giant loft apartment than a claustrophobic warehouse for cars. It was designed by Herzog & de Meuron, the noted Swiss architects behind the Tate Modern in London and Beijing's Bird's Nest Olympic stadium, and it shows. A grand staircase maneuvers down the center of the seven-story garage, creating the elegant aura of a European train station rather than a bland American parking structure. Beautiful sculptures and provocative works of public art dot the facility. High-end restaurants and boutiques (selling art books, handbags, footwear, high-concept athletic togs) are arrayed around the outside and on the top of the garage, while a fashion retailer occupies a striking eighteen-hundred-square-foot glass cube on the fifth floor.

In the morning, especially if it's raining, joggers and power walkers wind their way up and down the ramps of the facility, while yoga instructors teach classes on the top floors. Soon after it opened, couples began requesting that they be allowed to hold their weddings there, with one such black-tie ceremony written up in the *New York Times*. "When we saw it, we were in total awe," explained the blushing bride, who was an art gallery director. (Have you ever been invited to a wedding in a parking garage?) The couple was so enthusiastic, the *Times* reported, that they put an image of the garage on the invitations to their guests.

"The unique thing about eleven eleven is that it's really a curated space, not just a parking garage with retail," Robert Wennett explained to me as I tried to understand the "double vision" that allowed him to make his creative leap. "It's more like a cultural building than a commercial building. We actually 'program' the building. We help create events that people will talk about." For example, in true Miami style, Victoria's Secret did a commercial shoot directed by Michael Bay, the action-movie legend. Then Moncler, the French-Italian sportswear brand, celebrated its sixtieth anniversary by turning the seventh floor of 1111 Lincoln Road into a winter wonderland. "Here we are, it's eighty degrees, and they want snow because they're selling ski coats!" Wennett marvels. "What happens here on a daily basis is like a performance. You find things in places you don't expect to find them. You have experiences you don't expect to have. Nothing is what you expect. That's why people think it's so interesting."

Wennett and his colleagues always look for opportunities to do the unexpected, sometimes with subtlety, sometimes more brashly. Back when he bought the dispiriting property, it was home to a modest office building for SunTrust Bank, the financial services conglomerate based in Atlanta. When it came time to add a Sun-Trust branch to the reimagined complex, Wennett thought it made sense for the branch to have a drive-through option, despite its urban location, since it's part of a parking garage and Miami has such a car culture. But not just any drive-through. The facility is designed so that customers *drive through the bank itself*, with employees working on both sides of the line of cars. "When people think of drive-throughs, they think of an exterior space in the suburbs, where you're driving up to machines outside the bank," he says. "But here you drive through the actual bank. Can you conceive of that in New York City or any other urban place?"

Robert Wennett is justifiably proud of the mind-bending creativity behind 1111 Lincoln Road. "Everything about this project is not what it looks like on its face," he says. "It's not a parking garage, it's not an office building, it's not your normal retail space. We're creating an experience, we're telling a story." At the same time, he is adamant that the complex is a tough-minded business proposition, a high-performing commercial property, not just some "wild-and-crazy design statement" with no strategic rationale. In that sense, it embodies the brand of provocative competence championed by the brand builders at FCB. It is "thorough, smart, business-minded, and accountable," even as it is "challenging, surprising, restless, and imaginative."

It is, in other words, much more than an innovation. It is an act of imagination. "The reason this project is a great financial success is that it doesn't start with the finances," he explains. "It starts with the idea, a story with a soul." The essence of that story, he adds, is to invite visitors to encounter the unexpected. "In some ways the whole thing is quite bizarre," he notes. "We have a drive-through bank and a drive-up store! I have a house in a parking garage! But it's all part of creating an experience people have not seen before, with offerings in places where they have not seen them before. Nothing we do here is what you expect."

I got that same sense of the unexpected during my time canvassing in New Haven. I never asked Rosanne Haggerty if she plays trumpet or clarinet, or whether she is a fan of Miles Davis or Benny Goodman. But Frank Barrett's leadership lessons from jazz also do a virtuoso job of capturing the mind-set she embraced to overcome the paradox of expertise in her field. With Community Solutions, Haggerty and her colleagues developed an entirely new point of view about the most effective ways to solve the problem of homelessness, not just manage it, improvised a set of tools that allowed them to make measurable progress, and created a sense of urgency to deliver results faster than they'd ever been delivered before.

"I concluded, to my horror, that we had developed a way of attacking the problem that was inherently limited," she says about the business model she'd mastered at Common Ground. "It was good, it made a real contribution, but each of our initiatives took four or five years and could cost $40 million. That's what we were known for, that's what was unique. But the model couldn't scale. Our own blindness made me realize we needed a whole new way of looking at this issue. We had to blow ourselves up. I had to be willing to give up my identity as the 'Housing Lady,' someone who had spent years building and renovating facilities, and focus instead on optimizing existing housing resources."

By the time I found myself canvassing in New Haven, Rosanne

Haggerty, Becky Margiotta, and the 100,000 Homes Campaign had identified an array of strategies and tactics for getting to know a city's chronically homeless population and getting them off the streets. But this new business model emerged only after four years of affirmative moves, small disruptions, and a sharpening of perspectives—a collection of experiments in different places, with different techniques, from which the entire movement learned and grew. "It took me awhile to understand that this campaign was not about replication, copying what worked in one or two places," says Haggerty. "It was about adaptation, enabling communities to solve problems together, see things that we couldn't see, teaching us and everyone else what they were discovering."

By design, the 100,000 Homes Campaign went "out of business" on July 30, 2014. That was another insight that helped organizers overcome the paradox of expertise: If you want to break from the "homeless-industrial complex," you can't allow an initiative, no matter how effective, to go on forever. The existence of "term limits," the pressure to measure progress against a nonnegotiable outcome, creates the energy and creativity to meet the final goal and guards against a sense of creeping professionalism. Old-fashioned pressures around budgets, head counts, and long-term funding gave way to new obsessions with city-by-city timetables, Vulnerability Indexes, and "takedown targets"—the number of homeless people yet to be housed to reach the goal versus the number of days left to house them. "In this business, inertia is the same as negligent homicide for people on the streets," says Margiotta. "This campaign could not go on forever."

That does not mean, however, that the insights behind the movement don't endure. As soon as the 100,000 Homes Campaign wrapped up, Community Solutions unveiled its next initiative, called Zero: 2016.

The objective is for seventy-five participating cities to completely eliminate chronic homelessness by the end of 2016—that is, to get to absolute zero with a population that has been struggling for decades—within just thirty months after the campaign was first announced, as well as to end all homelessness among military veterans twelve months before that, by the end of 2015. It is a wildly ambitious goal, another social-change moon shot, but the sense of urgency and the level of boots-on-the-ground organizing and statistical detail behind the effort may well dwarf even what the 100,000 Homes Campaign was able to muster. Community Solutions and its allies vowed to "do whatever it takes to end veteran homelessness by the end of 2015 and end chronic homelessness one year later." I, for one, would not bet against them.

For their part, activists in New Haven (and elsewhere in the state of Connecticut) threw themselves into the new campaign with such vigor that they were prepared to declare victory on one of the goals earlier than planned. On August 27, 2015, Governor Dannel Malloy announced that the U.S. government had recognized Connecticut as the first state in the nation to have eliminated chronic homelessness among veterans, and that it was on its way to eliminating all veteran homelessness by the end of the year. (In February 2016, Malloy announced that the federal government had certified that Connecticut had "effectively ended homelessness" among all veterans.) What's more, Malloy agreed to the goal of eliminating chronic homelessness throughout the state of Connecticut, not just in greater New Haven, by the end of 2016.

The developments come as no surprise to Rosanne Haggerty;

it's what happens when you don't let what you know limit what you can imagine. "We see people reenergized about the possibility of actually solving these complex problems rather than just managing them," she says, as she reflects on her dramatic strategic shift since the early days of Common Ground. "We want to be the people who work ourselves out of a job."

Chapter 4

INTERESTING MATTERS, INTERESTED IS MANDATORY

"When's the Last Time You Did Something for the First Time?"

A while back, the *Wall Street Journal* published a brutally funny polemic against a word that has achieved mythical status among CEOs, business-school professors, and thinkers and writers like me—a word, I dare say, I've used too many times in this book already. That word is *innovation*. Dennis K. Berman, the *Journal* writer, began his withering account with a barb directed at Kellogg CEO John Bryant, the widely respected head of a global company that's been around since 1906. Bryant was describing one of the organization's noteworthy "innovations" for 2013. What was the game-changing, head-spinning breakthrough idea that Kellogg had unveiled? The Gone Nutty! peanut butter Pop-Tart. That's right, a world that has had to survive for decades with Pop-Tart flavors such as strawberry, raspberry, and cinnamon could now revel in the spirit of progress that delivered a Pop-Tart with peanut butter.[1]

Now, I would never dismiss the guilty pleasures of bad-for-you

breakfast foods, and it's hard to argue with the solid (if unspectac-
ular) performance of the Kellogg Company over the last century, or
even of the ubiquitous Pop-Tart since its debut back in 1964. But if
the CEO of a major global company can consider Gone Nutty! an
innovation, then what *isn't* an innovation? John Faraci, then CEO of
International Paper, admitted in the article that the word *innovation* "is way overused." As Berman put it, "Next time your boss starts
droning on about innovation, it might be helpful to stop and analyze: Is she talking about building the next iPod or the next Pop-
Tart?"

That's a thought-provoking question, especially for bosses who
aspire to build a more positive and provocative future for their
companies. It's so easy to pretend that trivial product tweaks and
modest brand extensions are a much bigger deal than they really
are. Or that launching a six-month "innovation program" or funding a low-budget "innovation department" is the same as unleashing a spirit of improvisation and experimentation that leads to
products and services that are, in the words of the FCB handbook,
"scary, challenging, and abruptive."

One telling (and depressing) case in point cited by Dennis Berman: When executives at Hewlett-Packard, a company starved for
exciting new products and clever strategic insights, held a Q&A
session with Wall Street analysts to discuss where HP was heading, they used the word *innovation* seventy times! (Sadly, HP has
become a poster child for the "permanently failing" organizations I
discussed in the prologue, a company that has survived for years
without exciting anyone.) What a contrast with the Tim Cook conference call I described in chapter 2 and his stirring message in

response to routine analyst questions about Apple's prospects. Why invoke an overused buzzword when you can summon a deeply felt set of beliefs about what the company stands for and what it's building for the future?

As I witnessed so memorably during my visit to Quicken Loans, words matter—in business, leadership, and organizational life. And when a word gets thoroughly misused and abused, it detracts from the very phenomenon it claims to describe and inspire. That may be why the most creative leaders I've met rarely use the "*i* word" to rally colleagues to their cause. It's too rote, too safe, too one-dimensional, too disconnected from the progress they hope to make and the risks they are prepared to take.

The most creative leaders rarely use the word *innovation* to explain their ambitions or inspire their colleagues.

Instead, they seemed to be embracing what strategist and jazz musician Frank Barrett likes to call "double vision"—the capacity to "act with confidence" in terms of what's always been done, "even as they are doubting, questioning, and probing their assumptions." Leaders with double vision "risk appearing unrealistic, even foolish, when they make the kinds of leaps that disrupt routines and create stretch goals—the kinds of leaps, that is, that provocative competence requires," Barrett notes. "The data to support such unusual moves simply doesn't exist, nor do the market indicators that would warrant changes in resource allocation and prioritization." Yet "without taking such leaps," he concludes, "companies and people remain stuck in the status quo."

Double vision, in other words, is about something more profound than small-bore projects to launch the next Pop-Tart or the newest laser printer. It goes to the nature of the creative process itself, to the personal qualities required to get beyond the paradox of expertise. Mihaly Csikszentmihalyi, the world-renowned psychologist, sociologist, and management theorist whose insights have shaped how so many of us think about motivation and performance, argues that truly innovative (sorry, that word again) artists, scientists, and executives embrace a set of internal paradoxes that form the "creative personality." What is the essence of the creative personality? "If I had to express in one word what makes [creative] personalities different from others, it would be *complexity*," he writes. "By this I mean that they show tendencies of thought and action that in most people are segregated. . . . Instead of being an 'individual,' each of them is a 'multitude.' Like the color white that includes all the hues in the spectrum, they tend to bring together the entire range of human possibilities within themselves."

Imposing stuff, to be sure, but when Csikszentmihalyi sets out a list of the paradoxical traits of the most creative people, he describes many of the entrepreneurs, change agents, and company builders we've met thus far, and speaks to the challenges of leadership going forward—the mind-set and outlook required to rethink what's possible in your field. For example, "creative individuals tend to be smart, yet also naïve at the same time," he writes. Brainpower is an essential ingredient of creativity, Csikszentmihalyi concedes, but brilliant people often "get complacent, and, secure in their mental superiority, they lose the curiosity essential to achieving anything new. . . . A certain immaturity, both emotional and mental, can go hand in hand with deepest insights." It sounds a lot like Liisa Joronen, a brilliant entrepreneur whose much-admired company was built on a naïve faith in what some of society's lowest-paid, lowest-status workers could achieve if they were given the chance to use their minds as well as their hands.

Creative people also demonstrate "a combination of playfulness and discipline, or responsibility and irresponsibility," Csikszentmihalyi asserts. "There is no question that a playfully light attitude is typical of creative individuals. . . . But this playfulness doesn't go very far without its antithesis, a quality of doggedness, endurance, perseverance. Much hard work is necessary to bring a novel idea to completion and to surmount the obstacles a creative person inevitably encounters." I can't think of a better way to describe Vernon Hill and the playful mind-set he brought to the challenge of building London's first new high street bank since 1835. Yet behind Metro's colorful, playful, sometimes goofy sensibilities is a sense of discipline and doggedness that incumbent banks simply can't match.

Here's one more: Creative individuals are "remarkably humble and proud at the same time," Csikszentmihalyi observes. "Another way of expressing this duality is to see it as a contrast between ambition and selflessness, or competition and cooperation. It is often necessary for creative individuals to be ambitious and aggressive. Yet at the same time, they are often willing to subordinate their own personal comfort and advancement to the success of whatever project they are working on." This language captures the spirit of Crosby and his colleagues at Pal's Sudden Service better than anything I could come up with. Spending time in Kingsport, Tennessee, I could sense the collective pride in the awards the company has won, the impact it has on the companies that come to visit and learn, and its status as a passion brand in the markets it serves. The people at Pal's know they've done something special and unusual. At the same time, they are humble about the fact that they can always do better, and have developed a system of teaching, coaching, assessing, and learning to maintain this deeply felt commitment to relentless improvement.[2]

I could go on with all ten of Csikszentmihalyi's insights about the "creative personality," each one more intriguing, compelling, *paradoxical*, than the next. But I hope the point has been made. There is so much more to the work of leading deep-seated, meaningful change, to overcoming the trade-offs and limits that define the sense of what's possible in most fields, than what can be addressed with the all-too-familiar language of innovation. Making a difference at your company or in your industry requires making sure that what you know doesn't limit what you can imagine.

"Creative people are constantly surprised," Mihaly Csikszentmihalyi concludes. "They don't assume that they understand what is happening around them, and they don't assume that anybody else does either. They question the obvious—not out of contrariness but because they see the shortcomings of accepted explanations before the rest of us do."

The most creative leaders are smart yet naïve, playful but disciplined, humble, and proud.

"WE ARE TRYING TO REINVENT THE INDUSTRY" —THE BIG COMPANY WITH A START-UP INSIDE

Commercial developer Robert Wennett and social activist Rosanne Haggerty, two of the undeniably creative personalities we met in chapter 3, don't have much in common other than their shared interest in (very different kinds of) real estate and the patterns of city life. Yet both of them, despite their records of tremendous achievement and well-established ways of doing business, overcame the paradox of expertise and built something original in their fields— acts of "calculated boldness" that went beyond anything they or their peers had done before. They display many of the paradoxical traits identified by Mihaly Csikszentmihalyi, and used those traits to devise all new strategies, brand-new metrics, exciting new stories, for what they were creating and the purpose they were serving. In the words of Cynthia Barton Rabe, they did not allow "the grounded reality of 'what is'" to interfere with their "'what-if' flights of fancy."

But what about the flip side of this all-important leadership challenge? Are there opportunities for knowledge and experience to become a platform for the future—not "millstones" to be shed, as Cynthia Barton Rabe warns, but cornerstones of a new wave of products, services, and offerings? Are there ways for leaders and organizations to let what they know, all the lessons they've learned, all the battles they've fought and the setbacks they've dealt with, *infuse* what they can imagine? The rise of Megabus.com, a colorful (and unlikely) force in the U.S. transportation market, points to some hopeful answers to these vexing questions.

Megabus is one of those game-changing outfits that's easy to describe but hard to appreciate unless you're in its target market. The company offers point-to-point bus service to and from 120 cities in North America. It launched in April 2006 with a hub in Chicago and express routes to Cincinnati, Indianapolis, Milwaukee, and five other Midwestern destinations. It took eighteen months for Megabus to go from launch to its millionth passenger, as it added buses, routes, and hubs. Over time, though, slow-but-steady expansion hit warp speed. It now does so much business (one million passengers every six weeks) in so many cities that analysts have coined a term to describe its impact on old-guard bus companies and the transportation system as a whole—the Megabus Effect. All told, in less than a decade, a single organization has modernized and elevated the image of bus travel, long dismissed as dowdy, dirty, and dangerous, and cultivated a wildly popular, fast-growing brand in a dull, slow-growth business.[3]

"This is new, different, unique," says Dale Moser, who has been responsible for Megabus since its launch in Chicago. "We are trying to reinvent the industry. This was an experiment, an initiative, a small bet on where travel could be heading. There was no 'guru' saying this is the future of bus travel. And we had no real competition. Our one true competitor is the car. The question we asked, and we didn't know the answer at the beginning, was, 'Could we get people out of their cars and onto our buses?' To do that, we had to reinvent the service and recast it."

There's no question that Megabus crafted an offering and an identity unlike anything that had come before it in its field. Sure, there are low-cost providers that connect highly traveled pairs of cities—Boston to New York, say, or Chicago to St. Louis—and a few national companies that have begun to offer lower fares on some routes that Megabus serves. But no offering combines point-to-point service, a national footprint, technology-infused reservations and ticketing, and such a colorful and playful brand personality. In July 2015, when CNN named its list of "11 People Changing the Way We Travel," the roster included Silicon Valley titan Travis Kalanick, founder of Uber; Fortune 500 executive Geraldine Calpin, global head of marketing and digital for Hilton Worldwide . . . and Dale Moser of humble Megabus.

What's really different about Megabus? Start with the buses themselves. Is there a less-appealing way to travel from, say, Dallas to Austin, or Pittsburgh to Cleveland, than on a cramped, run-down motor coach? But the distinctive Megabus is built for charm, convenience, and all kinds of creature comforts. The brightly colored double-decker buses are outfitted with oversized panoramic windows and a glass roof that make for great views. They also have electrical outlets at every seat, free Wi-Fi, and safety features such as three-point seat belts and GPS trackers to keep the buses on course and warn of low overpasses (an obvious concern with double-deckers). "The buses are one of the big drivers of the brand," says Dale Moser. "They're cool, kind of European, very environmental as well as economical. They're like moving billboards, you can't miss them. They look like no other buses on the road. They're our best form of advertising."

Then try the ticketing system. Does anything feel more antiquated, like you're a sad character in *Midnight Cowboy* or a fleeing perp on *Law & Order*, than waiting in line to buy a ticket in a dingy bus terminal? Megabus has a slick Internet-only reservation system built around the first yield-management software in the industry. Fares on each route start at one dollar (you have to book early to get one) and increase as the buses on a route fill up and the departure time draws near. (The company mascot, a caricature of a chubby bus driver that appears on the outside of every Megabus, is nicknamed One-Buck Chuck.) All tickets are paperless (reservations go directly to your phone or laptop) and all seats are guaranteed (some bus lines still sell as many tickets as they can and do their best to squeeze everyone on). There are premium seats (travelers pay extra to sit up front or up top) and, soon, there will be a luxury option with food and seats that recline into lie-flat beds.

Finally, check out the personality of the brand. For an old-school mode of transportation, Megabus has a pretty cutting-edge presence on social media. Partly because it's so popular with twentysomethings, partly because so many riders are online while they're onboard, passengers routinely post messages and images to their favorite social-media sites. College students traveling to the big game, bachelorette parties heading to the big city, even nervous guys popping the big question—they all get posted, tweeted, and shared. Megabus has six times as many Facebook fans as industry giant Greyhound, and a million addresses in its e-mail database.

"God bless the college students of America, they were the early adopters," says Mike Alvich, who served as the company's vice president of marketing when Megabus launched in 2006. "They'd try the service, tell their friends about it, tell their parents about it, and do it right from the bus since they were connected to the Internet. Our customers connect with us on Facebook, Twitter, Tumblr. This was a viral brand from the beginning."

Early on, to rally its first wave of enthusiasts, Megabus organized a grassroots marketing campaign with student ambassadors
on college campuses across the country. They'd show up at con-
certs, football games, and food festivals, and fly the company flag.
Today, students and young professionals are just one of the company's three primary constituencies. In fact, it has put together one of
the more unusual coalitions of customers I've come across. (Says
Moser: "We're creating new bus customers and a different demographic.")

The second big group of enthusiasts is single women traveling
together for a weeknight show or a weekend away who'd prefer not
to deal with driving. These customers also appreciate the fact that
in many of the cities it serves, Megabus uses its own downtown
pickup and drop-off spots rather than bus terminals, which still
have dubious reputations for safety. The third constituency is what
Megabus calls "silver surfers"—on-the-go senior citizens who love
a bargain even more than they love to travel. The older crowd tends
to buy well in advance and travel during periods when the younger
groups are at school or at work (mainly in the middle of the week).
"We're more than just a form of transportation," Alvich says. "We're
a passion brand, in a way. We let you do the things you like to do
in life."

Sometimes passion is more than a figure of speech. One of Alvich's favorite customer stories involves a frequent rider from New
York City who used Megabus to travel back and forth to Baltimore,
where his girlfriend lived. The guy, Avi Muller, decided to propose
marriage on the bus, which he considered a "lifeline" for his relationship with Nina Lazerow. So one Friday, with the help of the
company, Avi and an unsuspecting Nina hopped on in New York

with a busload of family and friends. Avi popped the question, Nina said yes, the bus erupted—and everything was caught on video. The moving proposal (pardon the pun) generated lots of reports on TV stations in New York City, caught the attention of *The Huffington Post*, and became a widely shared feel-good story. One account called it a "marriage made in Megabus heaven." For Alvich, it was manna from marketing heaven. The company ran a contest on Facebook called Megalove, in which customers posted their "long-distance love stories."

Quickly, quietly, and profitably, Megabus has become a force for renewal in an industry that has felt like a relic from the past, a breath of fresh air that has forced aging incumbents like Greyhound and Trailways to raise their game and modernize their strategies. Indeed, the Megabus story has all the elements of a blank-sheet-of-paper start-up, the kind of newfangled operation that gets hatched in a garage (appropriate for this industry) by a team of outsiders who see an opportunity to develop a whole new business model and challenge the existing power structure.

Except that Megabus was not the work of outsiders, and it is not a blank-sheet-of-paper start-up. It is, in fact, a young, nimble, progressive business unit of one of the biggest transportation conglomerates in the world, the new face of a multibillion-dollar giant that is about as established as it gets. Stagecoach Group, headquartered in Perth, Scotland, has annual revenues of $4.5 billion and 35,000 employees in the United Kingdom and North America. These employees operate 13,000 buses and trains that move millions of passengers every day, from local service in places like Dublin, Glasgow, Jersey City, and Bayonne to sightseeing tours, charter operations, even high-speed rail. All these businesses have their own histories, technologies, installed base, and talent pools. None has the strategy or brand sensibility of Megabus.

Which makes the rise of the new company all the more striking—and surprising. It's as if Delta or United, powerful airline incumbents, somehow gave birth to JetBlue or Southwest, "challenger brands" that transformed customer expectations and rewrote industry economics. Actually, after the rise of JetBlue and Southwest, Delta and United did try to create their own versions of these upstarts—to depressing effect. Delta unveiled Song, an obvious knockoff of JetBlue, in April 2003. The new business unit lasted barely five years. United launched Ted, its unoriginal twist on Southwest, in February 2004. Ted flew for about as long as Song. These lackluster attempts at strategic reinvention were yet another spin on the stories of CNN, MTV, and so many other case studies of the paradox of expertise. Delta and United had been doing business the same way for so long that they could not muster the will to do things differently—even when younger, faster-growing companies gave them a flight plan to success. They just couldn't match the commitment of the upstarts to combine lower fares with better service, higher efficiency with increased flexibility, no-frills operations with a more upbeat personality.

So how did Stagecoach Group do with Megabus what Delta and United could not do with their ill-fated start-up brands? How did the leaders of a giant conglomerate let what they know about their existing businesses inform their plan for a new business? Not by invoking a bunch of buzzwords, or creating a paint-by-numbers innovation program with budgets, committee reviews, and ROI calculations. In the spirit of Frank Barrett, the big-time success of Megabus is the result of small acts of improvisation, repetition, and disruptions to routine—none of which required huge investments, all of which required a kind of double vision that allowed executives to "act with confidence" as they were "doubting, questioning, and probing" their plans.

"I remember the day we decided we were going to start this weird new service," laughs Bryony Chamberlain, who was present at the creation, when Megabus ran its first routes from Perth, Scotland, to Edinburgh and Glasgow. "We had six weeks to set it up. We were going to use yield-management software, we had to build a Web site, we had to teach the drivers the routes, all while we did our day jobs. We wanted to juggle the market up and see what fell out—'Let's see how this might work.'"

That was back in 2004, after Stagecoach had closed down a business in China and brought back home a bunch of double-decker buses it had been using there. It was at a time when Ryanair, Europe's colorful and combative version of Southwest Airlines, was flying high and making headlines. Sir Brian Souter, the cofounder and longtime leader of Stagecoach, decided to experiment with his repatriated buses: Could he and his colleagues create a wheels-on-the-ground version of the low-cost point-to-point airlines, and thus invent a market where none had existed before?

The rest, as they say, is transportation history. Megabus grew quickly in Scotland, launched in England, then jumped across the Atlantic and opened for business in Chicago. (In the United Kingdom, the company mascot, the predecessor to One-Buck Chuck, is nicknamed One-Quid Sid.) The lightning-fast takeoff surprised even its most hopeful supporters. "The Web site cost us fourteen thousand pounds," Chamberlain says, chuckling. "The original vehicles were fully depreciated, cheap-to-run old double-deckers. We didn't expect it to do so well, we just wanted to try something, but suddenly we have this business growing like anything. It went from a wee little experiment to us running to keep up with customer demand because it was becoming such a major part of the company."

I didn't have to visit Scotland or England to spend time with Bryony Chamberlain, although her accent is so thick I felt like we should have been talking in a pub. She is based in Paramus, New Jersey, where she serves as director of operations for Megabus, but works out of the offices of Coach USA, the Stagecoach Group's five-thousand-person U.S. subsidiary. Mike Alvich served as director of marketing for both companies, and Dale Moser, as CEO of Coach USA, is responsible for Megabus as well. All three are adamant that Coach USA's long history and traditional operations have not interfered with the growth of their upstart brand. Quite the opposite. Megabus could not have grown as quickly and smoothly as it has, they argue, without the knowledge, savvy, and problem-solving skills of veterans who've been in the field for decades. It is one of the few examples I've encountered of a giant, incumbent organization being the first to develop a new line of sight into the future—and able to build a thriving new business based on those insights—without executives loyal to the old business standing in the way of progress.

"We have companies that have been running for seventy-five years," says CEO Moser, "people who have been working in the business for forty years. They've done it all, seen it all. This would have been dramatically more difficult if Megabus were an independent start-up. If we didn't have the infrastructure, the maintenance facilities, the safety systems, if we had to build all that from scratch, this whole thing would have taken three or four times longer than it has. It might not have even worked. This is the ultimate 'lean start-up,' even though it's part of a big company."

"WE ALL HAVE SOMETHING SIGNIFICANT YET TO DO" —THE LIFELONG QUEST FOR PERSONAL RENEWAL

More than a quarter century ago, at a high-powered gathering in Phoenix, Arizona, John W. Gardner delivered a speech that may be one of the most quietly influential speeches in the history of American business—a text that has been photocopied, passed along, underlined, and discussed by senior executives in some of the most important companies and organizations in the world. Gardner, who died in 2002 at the age of eighty-nine, was a legendary public intellectual and civic reformer—a celebrated Stanford University professor, an architect of the Great Society under Lyndon Johnson, the founder of Common Cause and Independent Sector. (I referenced his admiration for "tough-minded optimism" back in the prologue.)

Gardner's speech on November 10, 1990, was delivered to a meeting of McKinsey & Co., the consulting firm whose advice has shaped the fortunes of the world's richest and most powerful companies. But his focus that day was on neither money nor power. It was on what he called "Personal Renewal," the urgent need for leaders who wish to stay effective in a fast-changing world to commit themselves to continue learning and growing. Gardner was so determined that the message get through to the crowd that he wrote the speech out in advance "because I want every sentence to hit its target."

The central issue of his talk was "the puzzle of why some men and women go to seed while others remain vital all their lives." His puzzle came with a warning: "We have to face the fact that most men and women out there in the world of work are more stale than they know, more bored than they would care to admit. Boredom is the secret ailment of large-scale organizations. Someone said to me the other day, 'How can I be so bored when I'm so busy?' I said, 'Let me count the ways.' . . . Look around you. How many people whom you know well—people even younger than yourselves—are already trapped in fixed attitudes and habits?"

So what is the opposite of boredom, the outlook and mind-set that allows individuals to keep learning and growing, to escape fixed attitudes and habits? "Not anything as narrow as ambition," Gardner told the ambitious strategists. "After all, ambition eventually wears out and probably should. But you can keep your zest until the day you die." He then offered a maxim to guide the accomplished leaders in the room. "Be interested," he urged them. "Everyone wants to be interesting, but the vitalizing thing is to be interested. Keep a sense of curiosity. Discover new things."[4]

I can't think of a better lesson to draw from the acts of imagination we've encountered thus far in part 2, or a better maxim to guide the work of leadership going forward. Robert Wennett and his "coauthors" in Miami Beach, Rosanne Haggerty and her allies in the campaign against homelessness, Dale Moser and his colleagues at Megabus—all of them embraced a palpable zest for the future, a sense of curiosity and discovery that allowed them to move beyond their past achievements and break new ground. Their strategies for renewal—of a city, a cause, a mode of transportation—were informed by precisely the kind of personal renewal that John Gardner championed in his speech, and that eludes so many successful people in so many fields. What is the paradox of expertise, after all, other than a more polite term for the boredom about which Gardner warns, the "fixed attitudes and habits" that get in the way of learning and growth?

The most creative leaders I know are not just the boldest thinkers; they are the most insatiable learners. They work with unlikely partners (Olympic-level architects to design a parking garage), experiment with unusual tools (applying lessons from military intelligence to a social cause), borrow from new business models (translating the economics of low-cost airlines to the bus industry). It takes real commitment, especially after you've arrived at a position of power and responsibility, to push yourself to grow and learn, to question the ideas and assumptions that made your career in the first place. But that's what's required of leaders who wish to stay relevant. As interesting as they may be, they are determined to remain *interested*—in big ideas, in little surprises, in the enduring mission of their enterprise and all the new ways to bring that mission to life.

A few years back, Roy Spence, perhaps the most interested (and interesting) advertising executive I've ever met, published a book called *The 10 Essential Hugs of Life*, a funny and moving take on success. Among his wise and folksy pieces of advice ("Hug your failures," "Hug your fears," "Hug yourself") is a call to "Hug your firsts"—to seek out new sources of inspiration, to visit a lab whose work you don't really understand, to attend a conference you shouldn't be at, to rub shoulders with folks from different walks of life. "When you're a kid," he says, "every day is full of firsts, full of new experiences. As you get older, your firsts become fewer and fewer. If you want to stay young, you have to work to keep trying new things."[5]

Spence cites as one of his inspirations management guru Jim Collins, who, as a young Stanford professor, sought advice and counsel from none other than his learned colleague John Gardner. What did Spence learn from Collins (and, indirectly, from Gardner)? "You're only as young as the new things you do," he writes, "the number of 'firsts' in your days and weeks."

Garry Ridge, president and CEO of WD-40 Company, has built an entire organizational culture, and a style of individual leadership, around devising deeply held answers to John Gardner's (and Roy Spence's) deeply felt challenges. WD-40 may seem like a prosaic setting in which to wrestle with profound issues of leadership and learning, but Ridge and his colleagues have made some extraordinary commitments to maintain their zest for discovery, to stay interested in new ideas about products and purpose even as they work to make the company and its brands more interesting to the outside world.

The results speak for themselves. When Ridge took over back in 1997, WD-40 Company was a one-trick pony whose flagship product was iconic, beloved, even, a symbol of the do-it-yourself American spirit, but hardly the basis of a dynamic, exciting company. The multipurpose lubricant inside those famous blue-and-yellow cans was developed in 1953 to prevent corrosion on the metal skin of the Atlas nuclear missile. It took the chemist who developed it forty tries to perfect the water-displacement formula (hence the name WD-40), but once he got it right, it found applications far beyond the U.S.-Soviet arms race. Five years after this breakthrough in the lab, the company began selling its top-secret concoction in aerosol cans, and sales of the new multiuse product raced into the stratosphere. The company went public in 1973, and by the early 1990s WD-40's flagship offering was used in four of five American households and at virtually every mine, factory, and construction site in the country.

But WD-40's ubiquity limited its potential. Indeed, soon after Ridge took over, *Barron's* published an in-depth analysis called "The Cult of WD-40" that complained that "both the company and the stock" have "been going nowhere fast for some time." Ridge's company was so successful, yet so limited in its prospects, the magazine noted, that it was paying out almost 100 percent of its earnings as dividends to shareholders. "WD-40 is a cult product," *Barron's* proclaimed, but "it is hardly a cult stock." The "very nature of WD-40's past success doomed it to ultimate failure."

Which is precisely why Ridge, as the new CEO, set out to enrich the company's product portfolio, deepen its connections to customers, and broaden its identity. Its business was not water displacement or multipurpose lubrication, he told anyone who would listen. It was to "create positive lasting memories and solve problems in the workshops, factories, and homes of the world." The company's products didn't just keep things clean or free of rust, he insisted. Their job was to rid the world of "squeaks, smells, and dirt"—and thus make life a little more pleasant, and work a little less messy.

"Our products make heroes of people!" he exclaims. "If you have a squeaky engine, it's driving your family crazy, you solve that and everybody loves you. We're problem solvers and memory creators. And there are still many problems in many places we have yet to solve."[6]

"You're only as young as the new things you do, the number of 'firsts' in your days and weeks."

This lofty sense of strategic purpose, along with colorful packaging and clever marketing, catapulted the company into a second era of growth and prosperity, and turned it into a global passion brand. Today, its products are formulated in 13 factories and available in 176 countries and territories around the world. It has acquired a bunch of new brands (3-IN-ONE oil, Lava hand cleaner, Spot Shot carpet-stain remover, X-14 bathroom cleaner) that add to its arsenal for fighting squeaks, smells, and dirt. It has launched an array of WD-40 "specialist" products for professional users with particularly demanding needs. As for the original product, there are now WD-40 fan clubs in nearly every major country, homeowners and factory technicians who meet in person and online to share stories and swap ideas.

All told, the business is a well-oiled machine (pun intended). When Garry Ridge became CEO, 20 percent of the company's revenues were from outside the United States; today it's 65 percent. Its business in Europe alone is now bigger than its total revenues back when Ridge became boss. The share price has nearly tripled since 2009, and it has become, for the first time ever, a billion-dollar enterprise in terms of market value. (By the end of 2015, WD-40 shares were approaching $100 apiece and its market value was nearing $1.5 billion, unheard-of territory for the brand.) "We've unleashed the power of the shield," the CEO says, a reference to WD-40's signature logo. "Our blue-and-yellow can with the red cap is about only half the revenues it will eventually be. There are lots of squeaks in China and lots of rust in Russia. We're still a one-trick pony, but we define the trick differently."

There's no question that Garry Ridge has made WD-40 Company much more interesting than when he took over. But he did it by demanding that he and his colleagues become much more *interested* in what was possible for the company, its products, and the brand. Ridge overhauled the culture, redefined the work of its leaders, even embraced a whole new language, to put a premium on learning, experimenting, improvising—transforming a stale, insular business into something agile and open-minded. "Our true growth opportunity was to stop squeaks and smells all around the world. But people were afraid to step out of their roles. The fear of failure is the biggest fear in the world. We had to go from failure to freedom."

Ridge's most far-reaching move was to take a small group of executives, remove them from their day-to-day roles, and assign them to what he called Team Tomorrow. Their charter was to look far into the future (ten to fifteen years down the road) as well as to identify nearer-term trends (three to five years) and figure out what technologies the company would have to acquire, what tests it would have to run, what skills it would have to develop, in order to reimagine its existing products and imagine whole new lines of business. This was not some run-of-the-mill innovation project, the kind of committee that winds up recommending a new flavor of Pop-Tart. These were senior executives with backgrounds in strategy, marketing, finance, and R&D. Membership changed over time, but Team Tomorrow lasted for *ten years* and gave rise to a series of products, brands, and business strategies that will shape WD-40's prospects for years to come.

"The whole thing was inordinately successful," says Graham Milner, who held a series of high-level operating jobs at WD-40 Company before he was chosen to lead Team Tomorrow in 2002. Milner now runs WD-40 BIKE, a stand-alone company that offers a range of products (chain lubricants, foaming wash, frame protectants) for cycling enthusiasts in more than fifteen countries. WD-40 BIKE was just one of many ideas hatched by Team Tomorrow. The group also came up with the fast-growing WD-40 Specialist line, as well as a packaging breakthrough for the flagship WD-40 delivery system (the so-called Smart Straw, which has been a huge hit with customers). "Our job was to wake up every day and think about new sources of revenue for the future," Milner says. "It would never have happened if we also had day-to-day responsibilities for the present."

Garry Ridge disbanded Team Tomorrow in January 2012 after he concluded that responsibility for imagining the future could at last be folded back into the business. "If we want to help create positive lasting memories for our customers, we have to do the same for our colleagues," he explains. "How many parties have you left because you felt like you didn't belong? People want to be part of things where they feel comfortable, where they get a natural sense of growth and satisfaction. We're not just a company, we're a *tribe*, a tribe that puts a premium on meaningful work—work that means something to us, our customers, and the world at large. Those are the conditions under which talented people do magnificent things."

Ridge loves to invoke the language and spirit of a tribe to capture the sense of shared identity and mutual learning he aims to build. (It's also a neat twist on *tribology*, which, I learned to my surprise, is the technical term for the study of friction and lubrication.) The central ritual of "tribal" life at the company is what Ridge calls the "learning moment"—a period of frustration, a burst of inspiration, a breakthrough of collaboration in which people stumble upon a problem, unearth an opportunity, or fail miserably at an initiative, and then communicate what they've learned without fear of reprisal. He believes so strongly in the concept that he maintains his own Web site, TheLearningMoment.net, to share resources and perspectives with leaders from outside the company.

"Learning moments can be positive or negative, but they are never bad, so long as they are shared for the benefit of all," he says. "I want people to be inquisitive, I want people to ask questions and take chances. My job is to create a company of learners. I like to ask my people and myself, 'When's the last time you did something for the first time?'"

Ridge even insists that everyone at the company take the WD-40 Maniac Pledge, a solemn vow to become, in his words, a "learning maniac." (*Maniac* is second only to *magnificent* among this exuberant Australian's favorite words.) "I am responsible for taking action, asking questions, getting answers, and making decisions," it begins. "I won't wait for someone to tell me. If I need to know, I am responsible for asking. I have no right to be offended that I didn't 'get this sooner.' If I am doing something others should know about, I am responsible for telling them."

And on it goes, a formal statement of the mind-sets and attributes that transform leaders into learners—and that Ridge believes will allow him and his colleagues to keep transforming WD-40 Company. To underscore his personal commitment to the pledge, anytime he replies to an e-mail, he affixes an electronic signature with the message "Ancora Imparo," Italian for "I am still learning." The phrase was a favorite of Michelangelo's, according to the CEO, and the artist signed it into many of his works. (If he initiates an e-mail, it comes with an electronic signature that reads "We all have something significant yet to do," another favorite message to his colleagues.)

"One of my huge learning moments in life," Garry Ridge says, "was getting comfortable with those three magic words 'I don't know.' It's great to hear people across the company, anywhere in the world, say, 'I just had a learning moment' and share it with other people. Or to hear one of our people say 'Maniac Pledge'— knowing they have permission to ask about something they need to know or learn. My dream is for this organization to be viewed as a leadership and learning laboratory for business."

PART III

It's Just as Important to Be Kind as to Be Clever

Organizations that perform at a high level for a long time don't just think differently from everyone else, they care more than everyone else. In an era of big ideas and disruptive technology, simple acts of connection and compassion take on outsized importance.

Chapter 5

CIVILITY IS NOT THE ENEMY OF PRODUCTIVITY

"People Deserve to Be Treated Like People"

I had not planned to be spending the days before Thanksgiving thousands of miles from home, dining on reindeer stew and Alaskan Dungeness crab, and adjusting to fewer than seven hours of sun over the course of a day. But here I was, in Anchorage, on one of my final research trips for the book, eager to immerse myself in the leadership strategies, management practices, and customer-service lessons of what qualifies as something close to a medical miracle. This miracle is not a just discovered cure for cancer or an exciting new surgical technique. It was the top-to-bottom transformation of a dysfunctional and dispiriting health-care system into one of the most promising and progressive health-care systems anywhere in the country, if not the world.

I had come to visit with the leadership of Southcentral Foundation (SCF), a nonprofit health-care organization that runs the Anchorage Native Primary Care Center; comanages an affiliated 150-bed hospital, the Alaska Native Medical Center; and operates an array of specialized programs and facilities that serve an area larger than the state of Texas, a 108,000-square-mile region that stretches from Alaska's biggest city to villages in the Aleutian Islands accessible only by boat or plane. All told, the foundation delivers care to roughly 65,000 Alaska Native and American Indian people—a diffuse and disadvantaged population that has struggled for generations with sky-high rates of alcoholism, diabetes, obesity, and suicide.

In the bad old days, when the system was owned and operated by the Indian Health Service, patients routinely waited weeks for an appointment with a primary-care doctor, spent hours in crowded emergency rooms to get treatment even for minor ailments, and put up with a culture of care that could be condescending, rude, even downright cruel. The original hospital, which opened in 1953 as a tuberculosis sanatorium, added all kinds of services and specialties in subsequent decades, but it never quite shook the cold and indifferent atmosphere on which it was built. The situation was, in many respects, the worst of all possible worlds—the bloated costs of the U.S. health-care system, the glacial pace of a faraway federal bureaucracy, the desperate needs of a distinctly vulnerable group of patients.

Today, under what is called the Nuka System of Care, everything is different. (The word *nuka* means "big living things" in many indigenous Alaskan languages.) The system is owned and operated by Alaska Native people themselves. Nearly 55 percent of the total staff, 95 percent of the support staff, and more than 60 percent of the managers are Alaska Native, including many of the senior executives. The facilities are handsome, welcoming, open, and designed around the culture and art of the people they serve. There are spaces dedicated to traditional healing and "talking rooms" where people interact with doctors and nurses without all the clinical trappings. The emergency room is used to treat emergencies, not as a germ-filled sorting station for routine ailments.

Customer service is exceptionally responsive, by the standards of the health-care industry or any other industry, for that matter. People who ask to see a primary-care doctor are guaranteed same-day access, even if they make their request as late as 4:00 P.M., as long as they arrive by 4:30, and wait times average less than twenty minutes. No wonder employee-satisfaction ratings routinely hit 90 percent and customer-satisfaction ratings have reached as high as 96.9 percent. In a validation of its remarkable progress, SCF received the Malcolm Baldrige National Quality Award in 2011, the first non-hospital-centric health-care organization to win the prize.

Most notably, and most important, medical outcomes have gone from among the lowest in the country to some of the highest, even for hard-to-improve conditions such as asthma, diabetes, and infant mortality. A few decades ago, for example, Alaska's Native population had the worst results in the nation for infant mortality in the first twenty-eight days after birth. It now ranks among the best, a truly remarkable turnaround. Meanwhile, the percentage of diabetic patients with blood-sugar levels under control ranks in the top 10 percent of national standards. The percentage of children receiving high-quality care for asthma has increased from 35 percent of those who need it to 85 percent, and the rate of hospitalization for asthma patients has fallen from 10 percent to less than 3 percent.

The new definition of success for the Nuka System, its leaders have declared, is "a Native Community that enjoys physical, mental, emotional, and spiritual wellness." Their ultimate aim, they say, is "a Native Community that is renowned for being healthy." That's a far cry from what the community was renowned for over most of its history, and how the Indian Health Service defined success when it was in charge.

All of which explains why I'm not the first visitor to make this journey. In the last few years, hospital leaders and public-health officials from as far away as Scotland, Singapore, and New Zealand have trekked to Anchorage to see the changes for themselves and figure out what lessons they can apply. In 2015, the Harvard Medical School published a two-part case study on the strategies and tactics behind the transformation. When Donald Berwick, founder of the Institute for Healthcare Improvement and one of the world's foremost authorities on reform, visited Alaska in 2011, he called the system "the leading example of healthcare redesign in the nation, maybe in the world. It is an extraordinary gem. It can be the model for the reform of healthcare in America." The *New York Times* agreed. As part of a series on the future of health care, it devoted an entire Sunday editorial to the "astonishing results" in Alaska, noting its "startling efficiencies" and its potential to be "hugely inspirational" to other systems.[1]

So when I sat down with Katherine Gottlieb, CEO of Southcentral Foundation, who has been driving this transformation since 1991, I was bursting with questions about strategy and hungry for takeaways about leadership. (Back in 2004, Gottlieb won a MacArthur Foundation genius grant for her work as a change agent, the first person in Alaska to be so recognized.) How have she and her colleagues achieved such high levels of quality, consistency, and affordability, especially given the system's tortured past? How has the community made such dramatic progress on so many health challenges? What does she, as a CEO, consider her most effective techniques for recruiting allies to her reform agenda?

Gottlieb assured me that she and her colleagues would get to all my questions. (They've set up the Nuka Institute to share lessons with organizations from around the world, so there was almost no question they weren't prepared to answer, usually with detailed statistics and stacks of PowerPoint.) But first, she said, she wanted to "sit down and exchange stories, get a flavor for what we're bringing to the conversation." So we talked about my wife and kids, where I was born, what kind of background I came from. "While you're sitting here," she asked, "is your mind on your work or on your family back home?" We talked about why I cofounded *Fast Company*, whether I found it hard to write books (don't get me started), and how I wound up interested in health care in Alaska.

Then Gottlieb told me her story—in a way that was more visceral, more emotional, more *personal*, than that of any other CEO with whom I'd spoken. She was born in Old Harbor, Alaska, she said, a tiny village on Kodiak Island, to a Filipino father and an Aleut mother. She spent some of her childhood in Seattle, and then moved to Seldovia, a fishing village southwest of Homer. She is one of twelve siblings, the first in her family to graduate from college. She has six children, twenty-eight grandchildren, and four great-grandchildren. She began at the foundation back in 1987, when the entire organization had 24 staff members. She told the people who hired her that she wanted to be CEO: "They laughed and said, 'We have the perfect job for you—receptionist.'" So she began as the receptionist, but was put in charge just four years later, and has run things ever since. (SCF now employs more than 1,750 people.)

"My life experience comes from working in small communities, raising children, moving to Anchorage after village life," she told me. "Wherever I was, I wanted to change what I could change, improve what was around me. That's why I care so deeply about what happens here. I want this system to be sustainable for our children, and our children's children."

It was a unique and unexpected way to start an exchange of ideas, so I asked Gottlieb why she felt compelled to ask about my life and to tell me so much about hers. "If I don't know you and you don't know me, then how do we have a real conversation?" she replied. "So much of what we do here involves people being willing to share their stories, to open up about who they are and where they come from."

Physical health, she argued, begins with a strong sense of individual and group identity. "Wellness begins with being proud of your identity, recognizing that we as Alaska Native people own this system and this hospital," she told me. "The federal system treated us like numbers, like people who weren't worthy of something better. The walls were cracked, the hospital smelled terrible, you'd spend hours in the emergency room, and then be scolded by a doctor who was overworked and frustrated. So I knew I was going to change everything. *Everything*. But first and foremost, we knew that people deserve to be treated like people."

Hospital administrators who encounter the work of Southcentral Foundation can't help but focus on its astounding gains in productivity and efficiency—performance statistics that would be the envy of any health-care system in any major city. In recent years, emergency room visits per one thousand patients are down by more than 50 percent; hospital admissions are down by more than

40 percent; utilization of specialists is down by more than 60 percent; utilization of primary-care doctors is down by more than 30 percent. Annual staff turnover has fallen from more than 26 percent to 11 percent. The result of all these operating improvements is genuinely impressive cost control: Overall, even as the system has increased the number of people it serves by 7 percent, it has increased funding by just 2 percent.

Public-health officials who encounter the work of Southcentral Foundation can't help but focus on the dramatic advances in health and wellness among its population. Immunization rates for children in the system exceed 93 percent, higher than many places in the Lower 48, including tony neighborhoods in New York and Los Angeles, and especially impressive given that many kids live in remote villages. The C-section rate of 11.5 percent is one third the national average, also impressive as so many mothers in the system experience high-risk pregnancies. Its groundbreaking programs to combat fetal alcohol syndrome (the Dena A Coy Residential Treatment Program), adolescent mental-health problems (The Pathway Home), and domestic violence, child sexual abuse, and child neglect (the Family Wellness Warriors Initiative) have become models in their fields.

When I encountered the work of Southcentral Foundation I focused on something much more ordinary—and much more profound. Sure, when it comes to designing outpatient facilities and reinventing hospital operations, Katherine Gottlieb and her colleagues have devised breakthrough strategies from which change agents everywhere can learn. And, yes, when it comes to controlling costs and improving outcomes, they have found a positive-sum formula for which so many systems are still searching. But what makes their work so noteworthy, and so instructive, is that they recognize the limits of even the most clever thinking and the most disciplined execution. Ultimately, the leaders of SCF understand, the system they run will be sustainable, and the population they serve will be "renowned for being healthy," only if the people in it embrace a sense of identity that is as much about individual responsibility and personal transformation as it is about official policies and procedures. Their challenge is not just to manage the high-priced technologies and vexing trade-offs of modern medicine but to recognize and address the infinite mysteries of human behavior.

"They truly are pioneers," says researcher and consultant Cory Sevin, a nurse practitioner who serves as a director with the Institute for Healthcare Improvement and who describes herself as "a fan and a follower [of SCF] for a really long time." Sevin has advised health-care systems of all shapes and sizes, and she's clear about what separates the foundation from so many of the other systems with which she's worked. "They are so thoughtful about treating people as real human beings," she says, "and drawing on best practices in human-behavior change. Most systems are very physician oriented, or oriented around maximizing efficiencies for the system itself. They have done an amazing job of keeping a genuine human focus: deep listening about values and culture, understanding the barriers to becoming more vital in people's lives, serving people the way they want to be served rather than what's most convenient for the system or the staff."

Dr. Douglas Eby, SCF's vice president of medical services, who has been with the foundation since 1989 and has been a key figure in the development of the Nuka System of Care, explains the difference this way: "Modern medicine was hugely influenced by the scientific revolution, the industrial revolution, the assembly line. And for what it was created to do, address treatable diseases and fix broken things, modern medicine does miraculously well. But that's only about a third of what society now brings to the health-care system. We have basically medicalized life."

How so? "You used to go to the doctor for this much stuff," he replies, holding his hands a short distance apart. "But now you go to the doctor for *this much stuff*," as his hands sweep apart from each other. "But we've applied the same assembly-line model to everything that's being brought to health care: people who can't sit still, who can't socialize, who are chronically overweight. Traditional diagnosis, prescriptions, and treatment plans are truly secondary to that work, which is now two thirds of the work we're being asked to do. Whether people take their meds, eat well, lash out violently—that's almost entirely controlled by them, not by us. So our main work is to influence people and give them tools to be responsible for their health, to walk with them over time on their own journey to wellness. That's why we have to do something different."

That "something different" shapes everything SCF does: how it designs its facilities, who serves on its much-studied integrated-care teams, why it makes such extensive and unprecedented use of so-called behavioral health consultants (BHCs) and trains virtually everyone on its staff, right down to dental assistants, on how to recognize the warning signs of addiction, depression, or domestic abuse, and respond immediately. "The whole system is on guard for mental-health and behavioral issues," says Chanda Aloysius, an Alaska Native (Athabascan Indian and Yupik Eskimo) who, like

Katherine Gottlieb, started out as a receptionist and now serves as the system's vice president of behavioral services. Of the sixty-five thousand customer-owners in the system, fully 50 percent will have a "diagnosable behavioral-health event in their lifetime," Aloysius estimates.

SCF's human-centered outlook even shapes the language it uses to describe the population it serves. For example, and this doesn't roll trippingly off the tongue, everyone at SCF calls their patients customer-owners rather than patients, and wants their patients (sorry, customer-owners) to refer to themselves the same way. Just once during my many interviews and meetings with managers and staffers in Anchorage, I was hoping someone would use the word *patient* as shorthand, if only to simplify our discussions or provide a "gotcha" moment. Alas, it was not to be.

Why this commitment to a rather awkward piece of language? To raise everyone's standards for the system—and themselves—about how they should expect to be treated and what they should expect for their lives. "We want people to live and breathe ownership of their health," says Katherine Gottlieb. "We don't want to be the heroes who come in and cure you. We want our customer-owners to say, 'I am responsible for my own health and healing, and you are my chief adviser.'"

That same responsibility, she notes, applies to the foundation itself, and the remarkable fact that Alaska Native people now own and operate a system that for decades, in her words, "treated us like cattle." When that prominent *New York Times* editorial shined a spotlight on the Nuka System of Care, Gottlieb celebrated its publication. She wasn't looking to draw attention to herself (she's one of the most self-effacing CEOs I've met), but to make sure the foundation's customer-owners understood just how far they'd come, as well as their responsibilities going forward. "You are on the map," she told them. "People from around the world are coming here to learn what you've done. You're changing global health care." All this progress, she added, comes with a challenge: "You are responsible for your health, you cannot rely on doctors to make you well. But you are also responsible for your health-care system. You own it! So if you don't like something, change it."

"DO SMALL THINGS WITH GREAT LOVE" —WHY IS IT SO HARD TO BE KIND?

As I've argued throughout this book, much of the business culture is obsessed with big ideas, disruptive innovations, and one-of-a-kind strategies for change—the edgy, exciting material that fuels our competitive juices, hones our strategic edge, and (hopefully) makes for page-turning reads. But sometimes the simplest stories can teach the most important lessons about success, leadership, and life—especially when those stories remind us that great advances in creativity and productivity should never come at the expense of empathy and generosity. To be sure, the world confronts vast uncertainty, from unrest in the social climate to worrisome changes in the climate itself. The global economy is experiencing a deep-seated transformation, from unsustainable concentrations of wealth to the convulsive impact of computing and communications. But it is precisely during periods of such enormous upheaval that small acts of connection capture our attention and imagination. "Not all of us can do great things," Mother Teresa famously said. "But we can do small things with great love."

Consider this heartwarming story about a young man, his dying grandmother, and a bowl of soup, and what it says about the future of service, brands, and the human side of business—the virtues of doing small things with great love. The story, as told in *Adweek*, goes like this: Brandon Cook, from Wilton, New Hampshire, was visiting his grandmother in the hospital. Terribly ill with cancer, and undergoing yet another bout of treatment, she complained to her grandson that she desperately wanted a bowl of soup, but the hospital's soup was inedible (she used saltier language, not suitable for a family-friendly book). If only she could get a bowl of her favorite clam chowder from Panera Bread! Trouble was, Panera sells clam chowder only on Fridays—a legacy, I'm guessing, of old-school New England Catholicism and a history of meatless Fridays. So Brandon called the closest Panera, talked to the store manager, a woman named Suzanne Fortier, and explained his dilemma. Problem solved: Not only did Sue and the staff brew up a fresh batch of clam chowder especially for Brandon's grandmother, they included a box of cookies as a get-well gift.

It was a simple gesture of support that would not normally make headlines. Except Brandon wrote up the story on his Facebook page, and his mother, Gail Cook, reposted his write-up (after a few edits) to Panera's Facebook wall. It was nothing particularly deep or poetic, just a short review of the situation ("My grandmother is passing soon with cancer . . ."), a description of what Sue and the staff did ("Without hesitation she said she would make her some clam chowder . . ."), and a genuine statement of thanks ("It's not that big a deal to most, but to my grandma it meant a lot . . .").

The rest, as they say, is social-media history. Gail's post on Panera's Facebook page generated nearly 810,000 "likes" and more than 35,000 comments—an outpouring of gratitude and recognition for Brandon's grandmother, Sue and her colleagues in Nashua, and the company for which they worked. Meanwhile, Panera, one of the great retail growth stocks of the last fifteen years, got something no amount of advertising could buy. A company whose shares appreciated forty-five-fold between 2000 and 2015 won a sense of appreciation and affiliation from customers around the world who were moved by the spontaneous actions of a single person.[2]

"My family is eating at Panera tonight because of this story," a commenter from Pontiac, Michigan, wrote. "Way to go Sue and Panera!" Added a commenter from Elkton, Maryland, "There are still good people in this world." A commenter from Sinking Spring, Pennsylvania, wrote: "Amid pain and suffering and a need for some kindness, it was found. God bless Sue and Panera and God bless Brandon and his dear grandmother!"

Marketing types latched on to the story as an example of the powers of social media and online word of mouth to boost a company's reputation. (It came to prominence in *Adweek*, after all.) But I see the reaction to Sue Fortier's gesture to a hungry cancer patient as an example of something else—a genuine hunger among customers, colleagues, and the rest of us to engage with organizations that are prepared to recognize us as individuals and do a little extra to make us feel special. In a world that is being reshaped by technology, what so many of us crave, what truly stands out, are small gestures of kindness that remind us of what it means to be human. Indeed, when a local New Hampshire news site tracked down Brandon and asked him about the outpouring of emotion on Facebook, he talked about the deeply personal impact of this virtual show of support. "If my grandma even knew what a Facebook page was, I'd show her," he cracked. "My grandma's biggest fear was dying with no friends. I wish I could show her how many 'friends' she has out there, and how many prayers people are saying for her."

In fact, the more I learned about the Panera Bread story, the more I was reminded of an experience of my own back when my father turned seventy-five and I wanted to give him a special gift to mark the milestone. How does a dutiful son do something nice for his dad? Why, he buys him a Cadillac, of course! So I called my father, whose ten-year-old Cadillac was showing its age, and gave him the news: You visit the showroom, pick the model, negotiate the price, and I'll do the rest.

He was thrilled. So he drove his old car to the dealer, test-drove the new models, chose the options he wanted, and started talking price. Toward the end of that discussion, he reminded the dealer that he'd received a one-thousand-dollar customer-loyalty discount in the mail, which he planned to apply to the car. This was on a Friday afternoon. Turns out, the dealer told him, the loyalty discount had expired—on Thursday, less than twenty-four hours before the visit. "But I assume you'll honor it anyway," my father said. "I've been a faithful customer." Sorry, the dealer told him, but the terms are the terms.

Needless to say, that unexpected reaction stalled the conversation. My father drove away, a little confused and more than a little disappointed, and decided to look around more—not at other

Cadillac dealers, but at other brands. The next Friday, he drove by a Buick dealership and decided to stop in. A Buick LaCrosse caught his eye, and he struck up a conversation with the dealer. (The La-Crosse, it turns out, had emerged as a super-popular model with the sixty-five-and-over set. Who knew?) He told the story of his loyalty certificate. The dealer checked the computer and confirmed that it had indeed expired. "But no problem," he said, "we'll honor it. We'll knock a thousand bucks off whatever price we agree to." Impressed, my father decided to take the LaCrosse for a ride. He liked the experience, but told the dealer he wished he had stopped by earlier in the day, so he could drive it longer. "Then take the car for the weekend," the dealer said. "Bring it back on Monday and we'll go from there."

It was a great plan, until Monday rolled around and my father found himself being rushed not to the dealer but to the hospital, with what turned out to be a medical problem that required sur-gery. (He came through with flying colors.) As he was lying in his hospital bed, thinking about whatever it is we think about in those quiet moments, he realized the Buick LaCrosse was sitting in his garage! So he called the dealer from the hospital and asked how he could get the car back. "Don't worry about the car," he said. "Just get better." And the next morning, what should arrive at the hospital but a lovely bouquet of flowers and a nice note from the Buick dealer!

So here's a question: Which car did my father buy? If you said the Buick LaCrosse, you would be correct. Here's a second ques-tion: For more than a year after that purchase, what was one of my father's favorite topics of conversation with friends, associates, and just about anyone he came in contact with? If you said the incredible treatment he received from the Buick dealer (as opposed to the hospital, which saved his life), you'd be correct again. Forget Facebook: Those flowers triggered a word-of-mouth campaign that would be the envy of marketers everywhere.[3]

In a world being reshaped by technology, what so many of us crave are small gestures of kindness that remind us of what it means to be human.

Now here's the real question: Why is it so rare for businesspeople to behave like the Buick dealer, and so common for businesspeople to behave like the Cadillac dealer? It remains a mystery to me, but there's nothing mysterious about the results of those contrasting behaviors. Nobody is opposed to a good deal—a dollars-and-cents value proposition, as we discussed in chapter 1. But what we tend to remember, what we appreciate, what we *prize*, are gestures of concern and compassion that introduce a touch of humanity into the all-too-bloodless calculations that define so much of twenty-first-century commerce and modern life. Not always a head-turning, one-of-a-kind values proposition of the sort pioneered by Metro Bank or 1111 Lincoln Road, but just enough civility and decency to represent a welcome alternative to standard operating procedure.

The evidence is all around us. Imagine my fascination, as someone who believes in the power of small gestures to send big signals, when the front page of the *New York Times* carried a report on a "broad and transformative trend" that was sweeping Russia. It had nothing to do with more democracy, less corruption, or a turn away from military adventurism. It had to do with simple ideas about customer service—specifically, an intense focus inside Aeroflot, the famous (infamous, really) airline, to teach flight attendants how to connect with their passengers as human beings. "Gone are the scowls, the cold shoulders and the wordless encounters" that had defined the Aeroflot experience, the *Times* reported. In their place were appeals for warmth, pleasantries, and, gasp, smiles. The result was "a mini Velvet Revolution for a region accustomed to old ideas of Russian service."

In the old days, the article noted, flight attendants received training from choreographers with the Bolshoi Theatre on "stride and movement"—the better to display their admire-from-a-distance beauty and unapproachable elegance. Now the focus is on making conversation, striking up personal interactions, being nice to customers who don't expect it. "Anna, you just showed her the champagne bottle but didn't say anything," one instructor coaxed a trainee. "This is the silent service of Soviet times. You need to talk to her. And you need to smile and smile and smile."[4]

I found two things especially noteworthy about this report. First, these ridiculously simple reminders have had a huge impact inside Aeroflot. According to the *Times*, customer surveys indicate that the airline has the best-ranked service of any carrier in eastern Europe, including Western airlines and their partners who operate in the region. Second, Aeroflot's program was gaining altitude at a time when the business culture in the United States and Europe seemed to be questioning the value of human-to-human connections. In an era of cutthroat competition, deep-seated cynicism, and the digital disruption of everything, who wants to make big bets on the power of small gestures? Not very many organizations, it seems, which is why stories like that of the concerned Panera store manager or the kindhearted Buick dealer seem so few and far between. Civility is not the enemy of productivity—although far too many companies and their leaders act as if it were.

"CATCH PEOPLE IN THE ACT OF DOING THINGS RIGHT" —THE REAL WORK OF EMOTIONAL LABOR

Indeed, some months before my eyes were opened by the *Times* report on the changes at Aeroflot, my head was sent spinning by an outburst of snide, almost contemptuous, accounts of the success of Pret A Manger, the fast-casual sandwich shop headquartered in London, and its unapologetic commitment to developing a workforce that is bright, cheerful, and happy to keep smiling. (In a way, Pret A Manger is to the United Kingdom what Panera Bread is to the United States.) I've been following Pret for almost fifteen years, after we published an article in *Fast Company* about the upstart British chain's push to enter the American market. That piece appeared in 2002, and the company's growth since then has been impressive. Back in 2002, Pret had 118 locations in the United Kingdom, 5 in New York, and 1 in Hong Kong. By 2014 it had 374 locations around the world, with more than 60 in the United States (in four different cities), not to mention Paris and Shanghai as well, that serve well over 300,000 customers per day.

One defining element of the Pret business model is its wide

variety of fresh premade sandwiches. (The company's name means "ready to eat" in French.) This approach allows customers to get in and out of the store in as few as sixty seconds, a truly make-or-break benefit for harried office workers, its target market. But Pret wants even that brief time in its shops to be filled with smiles, positive energy, and a genuine human connection, especially for repeat customers. CEO Clive Schlee calls it the Pret Buzz, and the company has identified a set of Pret Behaviors to create the buzz. "We only employ people who are friendly and lively," company policy states, "people who are good-humoured by nature." When Schlee visits a store, he told a reporter from London's *Telegraph* newspaper, he immediately sizes up how employees are interacting with one another, not just with customers. "I can almost predict sales on body language alone," he said.

The company has a rigorous training program to instill its Pret Behaviors in the company's frontline employees, an initiative called the Pret Academy, along with a staff manual that describes the atmosphere it hopes to create. (This is, it should be emphasized, a remarkably multicultural phenomenon. Pret's employees in the United Kingdom come from 106 different nationalities, and only 18 percent of them are British. Other leading nationalities are Poles, Colombians, and Italians.) The manual "tells staff to 'use personal phrases that you are comfortable with and treat customers as if they are guests in your own home,'" the behind-the-scenes report in the *Telegraph* explains. "This is nothing so glib as a 'Have a nice day' culture; this is a philosophy that runs much deeper."

It's also a philosophy that has attracted loud critics on both sides of the Atlantic. The first attack I saw came from an essay in the *London Review of Books*, which objected to the very idea that

Pret employees should be expected to do more than serve decent food at a good price. "What Pret has understood, and its competitors haven't (or not yet), is how much money there is to be made from what radical left theorists have been referring to since the 1970s as 'affective labour,'" the essay argued. "Work increasingly isn't, or isn't only, a matter of producing things, but of supplying your energies, physical and emotional, in the service of others. It isn't what you make, but how your display of feelings makes others feel. This won't be news to mothers, nurses, and prostitutes, but the massive swelling of the service economy means that emotional availability can no longer be dismissed as women's work; it must be seen as a dominant commodity form under late capitalism." (*Phew.* If only Karl Marx were here to analyze the means of production behind the classic cheddar and tomato sandwich.)

One month later came an assault in the *New Republic* by Timothy Noah, who offered his own withering (albeit less dialectical) critique of the "emotional labor" and "enforced happiness" that is at the heart of the Pret model. The essay began with a personal lament (tongue in cheek, I hope, for his sake) about how Noah had come to believe that a young employee (a "slender platinum blonde") behind the counter at his local Pret was in love with him. "How else to explain her visible glow whenever I strolled into the shop for a sandwich or a latte?" he asked. "Then I realized she lit up for the next person in line, and the next. Radiance was her job." Noah then generalizes from his personal disappointment. "Why must the person who sells me a cheddar and tomato sandwich have 'presence' and 'create a sense of fun'?" he wonders. "Why can't he or she be doing it 'just for the money'? I don't expect the swiping of my credit card to be anybody's vocation. This is, after all, the economy's bottommost rung."

Noah is entitled to his crotchety point of view, but it strikes me as both odd and condescending to think that frontline service jobs should be performed with a grim sense of duty and bare-bones competence. Isn't it better for customers, and for employees, to be part of an atmosphere that is built around good cheer and personal expression rather than gritted teeth and furrowed brows? That's one reason Pret has resisted using loyalty cards, those frequent-purchaser programs that entitle customers to a free coffee or sandwich after they do a certain amount of business with the chain. Instead, frontline employees have the authority (in fact, they're required) to offer customers free drinks and menu items, not just to make up for mistakes but to recognize a nice gesture from an upbeat customer or to lift the spirits of someone who looks to be having a tough day. "The staff have to give away a certain number of hot drinks and food every week," CEO Clive Schlee explained. "They will decide, 'I like the person on the bicycle' or 'I like the guy in that tie' or 'I fancy that girl or that boy.' It means 28 percent of [customers] have had something for free. It's a nice, different way of doing it."[5]

To be sure, the Pret experience is not for everybody. Which is why Pret evaluates job applicants based on how well their personal values map to the company's core behaviors, and assigns them to work trial runs at a shop before they're hired, after which current employees vote on whether to extend a full-time offer. (The employees reject about 10 percent of the candidates.) In other words, who you are as a person counts as much as what you know at any moment in time at an organization like Pret; your character counts as much as your credentials. Indeed, every high-energy organization I've encountered makes it clear to all concerned: If you don't fit, it's going to be hard for you to commit.

I'm convinced that "emotional labor" will become a more important job of companies that win big in the future, and that's a phenomenon that makes me smile. So I pose the question again, this time in more general terms: What is it about business that makes it so hard to be kind? And what kind of leaders have we become when small acts of connection feel so uncommon? Somehow, without ever intending it, organizations of all shapes and sizes have managed to eliminate the spontaneous expression of positive emotions, simple acts of decency, from their day-to-day operations. They're not rewarded, they're not celebrated, they're not taken seriously, even when it's clear that colleagues, customers, and all sorts of other constituencies value them. Is it really that difficult for organizations and their leaders to think and act in ways that bring out the best in everyone they encounter?

Ward Clapham is a leader who wrestled with that very question, even though his "business" is built on the worst of what people have to offer. When he took command of the Royal Canadian Mounted Police in Richmond, British Columbia, the third largest force in the country, he faced a problem with juvenile delinquency and crimes (some serious, some petty) committed by alienated young people. One of the basic "realities of my job," he wrote in *Breaking With the Law*, was that he and his fellow Mounties had to "hunt down criminals" as a normal part of doing business. But Clapham wasn't satisfied with just being tough on crimes after they were committed. Might there be a way to engage troubled young people on more positive ground, to celebrate them for doing the right thing rather than always punishing them for doing the wrong thing? Could he transform a "service business" based on negative interactions into something more positive?

His answer was an innovation he called "positive tickets." Of course his officers cited and arrested kids for breaking the law. But they also went out of their way to find at-risk kids who were staying out of trouble, who were doing small positive things at a skate park, or at school, that were making life a little better for them and the people around them. At those moments, he and his officers issued positive tickets—citations that entitled the recipient to a free meal at a restaurant, or free admittance to a movie or a theme park. "Instead of catching kids doing something wrong," he explains, "positive ticketing is about catching kids doing something right."

It's also about changing the attitudes and mind-sets of frontine personnel. "Catching kids doing good things is fun," he told his colleagues, and the officers who do it "should have fun with it. Does this mean you have to do a circus act every time you hand out a ticket? Of course not. But youth can see right through a façade. If adults are not truly interested in kids' good behavior, if they are handing out tickets just to fill a specific quota, or if they would rather be doing something else, the kids will know immediately. Handing out positive tickets should be the best part of your day, and your face and demeanor should reflect it."

Clapham and his colleagues issued roughly 40,000 positive tickets per year—three times as many citations as they issued for violations. "I guess you could say we were still the hunters," he wrote, "but now we were hunting for good behavior." As a result, he reports, youth-related service calls to the department dropped by

50 percent, and an estimated 1,000 young people stayed out of the criminal-justice system. More to the point, the very nature of the relationship between the police and the community changed. "The part that makes it worthwhile is pulling into a parking lot full of kids," he writes. "Instead of running away from me, they swarm me.... Kids don't feel I am hunting them anymore; they see me as a friend."[6]

What is it about business that makes it so hard to be kind? What kind of leaders have we become when small acts of connection feel so uncommon?

Even a no-nonsense leader like Internet billionaire Jeff Bezos has been forced to wrestle with the virtues of a bighearted outlook on work and life, and the power of small gestures to reinforce or detract from that outlook. Awhile back, the aggressively competitive, take-no-prisoners founder of Amazon.com delivered a memorable baccalaureate address to the graduating seniors of Princeton University (my alma mater). Bezos is nothing if not a master of strategy and technology. But on this important day he spoke not about drone deliveries or cloud computing but about a painful encounter with his grandmother, and what he learned when he made her cry.

Even as a young boy, it seems, Bezos had a steel-trap mind and a passion for numbers. During a summer road trip with his grandparents, Jeff got fed up with his grandmother's smoking. From the backseat, he calculated how many cigarettes per day she smoked, how many puffs she took per cigarette, the health risk of each puff, and announced to her, "You've taken nine years off your life!" The reaction that followed was not what he anticipated. "I expected to be applauded for my cleverness and arithmetic skills," he said. Instead, his grandmother burst into tears. His grandfather, who had made no comment on the conversation, pulled over to the side of the road, got out of the car, and invited Jeff to get out too: "My grandfather looked at me, and after a bit of silence, he gently and calmly said, 'Jeff, one day you'll understand that it's harder to be kind than clever.'"

I realize that Jeff Bezos may be an unlikely voice to deliver this heartfelt message. In the summer of 2015, the *New York Times* published an explosive and controversial front-page examination of the ferociously demanding, sometimes downright brutal workplace culture inside Amazon. Years earlier, it turns out, Bezos had begun to reckon with the question of how Amazon—so hard-charging, ambitious, and relentless—was being perceived by the world. He actually wrote a memo to his senior colleagues, titled "Amazon.love," that posed the question of whether the company, when it hit $100 billion in annual sales (the number was $89 billion in 2014), would be feared or loved. "Some big companies develop ardent fan bases, are widely loved by their customers, and are even perceived as cool," Bezos wrote, identifying Nike, Costco, and UPS among this group. Others, he noted, including Walmart, Microsoft, and Goldman Sachs, occupy the other end of the spectrum, which is where he did not want Amazon to be.

How a company is perceived, Bezos concluded, largely came down to how it behaved, and how its behaviors compared with those of its direct competitors. "Rudeness is not cool," he warned his colleagues. "Defeating tiny guys is not cool," he added. "Polite is cool," he argued, "defeating bigger, unsympathetic guys is cool." There was more. "Explorers are cool," he said, "conquerors are not cool." And, in a nod to John Doerr, who helped finance Bezos's company and served for years on Amazon's board of directors, "Missionaries are cool. Mercenaries are not cool."[7]

Yes, the most effective leaders urge their colleagues to embrace advanced technology, reimagine what's possible in their industry, seek out new ideas from the widest variety of sources, and exude a will to win. But they also make sure that the drive for creativity and productivity doesn't come at the expense of individual (and organizational) capacity for compassion and generosity. As he wrapped up his speech to the Princeton students, Bezos posed twelve questions to the graduates that captured what he had learned over the course of his life and career, including "Will you follow dogma, or will you be original?"; "Will you wilt under criticism, or will you follow your convictions?"; "Will you play it safe, or will you be a little bit swashbuckling?" But it was the final question that was the most autobiographical, the one still yet to be answered inside Amazon itself, and the most important for aspiring leaders everywhere: "Will you be clever at the expense of others, or will you be kind?"

Chapter 6

THE TOUGH-MINDED CASE FOR LEADING WITH LOVE

"We Want People to Know What True Happiness Feels Like"

Kevin Roberts, the long-tenured CEO (now executive chairman) of Saatchi & Saatchi, and one of the most endearing advertising minds of his generation, has coined a term to describe the potential for companies to forge bonds of emotion and affiliation with their customers. Trademarks are obsolete, he argues. The new goal should be to create "lovemarks"—brands that become a "beautiful obsession" and create "loyalty beyond reason," the kind of deep-seated connections "that can forgive lapses and understand failure." Take away a traditional brand, Roberts says, and most people will find a replacement. "Take away a lovemark," he adds, "and people protest."

Why are there so few lovemarks in a marketplace bursting with products, services, and brands with sleek designs and huge advertising budgets? Because, Roberts argues, too many companies focus too narrowly on the details of price, performance, and features when they explain their offerings to customers.

Lovemarks—"charismatic brands that people get emotional about"—revel in "mystery, sensuality, and intimacy." They aren't built through expensive TV spots or clever social-media campaigns, he says, they require "a new point of view. A way to change how companies see themselves and how they feel about consumers. And, as importantly, how consumers feel about business." The message for senior executives and the organizations they lead: "Love is here to stay. . . . Why would we discard emotions in business when they play such a central role in our daily lives? The same human impulses that create passionate connections in our families and friends are the very ones we need at work."[1]

I love how Kevin Roberts's mind works, and I have no doubt that he is onto something big with his passion for lovemarks. Still, the more I reflect on the global outpouring of affection for Panera Bread, or how a kindhearted Buick dealer won a customer for life, the more I appreciate that leaders who aspire to do big things can't lose sight of the small things that make such a huge impression inside and outside the organization. In an era of radical ideas, disruptive technology, and big-budget marketing, simple acts of connection take on outsized importance. You can't quantify it on a spreadsheet, but there is a tough-minded case for leading with love.

I can't make the case for the power of small gestures to send big signals, the virtues of leading with love, without revisiting the case study of Southcentral Foundation and its impact on the health of its population. SCF is nothing if not a lovemark—an organization that inspires "loyalty beyond reason" among employees and customer-owners alike. But as Katherine Gottlieb emphasizes, the huge strides that she and her colleagues have made are the sum total of countless one-on-one encounters, personal messages, and small interventions to engage people as the distinct, complex, flesh-and-blood human beings they are. What distinguishes the leadership strategies behind the Nuka System of Care, what separates it from by-the-book, numbers-driven programs to manage costs and improve outcomes, is the consistent and creative focus on how to understand and influence what makes people tick, not just how to get people well when they're sick.

That leadership focus began long before Gottlieb became CEO. In fact, it began shortly after she was hired as a receptionist. As a newcomer to the small, resource-starved organization, she was disappointed with the drab walls, shabby furniture, and haphazardly dressed colleagues that were part of her daily surroundings. How could patients (they weren't "customer-owners" yet) feel good about themselves and their health when the facility they visited looked like it was on life support? So Gottlieb took it upon herself to paint the walls, change out the rugs, install a handsome oak desk, and dress in ways that made a thoroughly professional impression.

"The reason to change the surroundings," she told me, "was to change the attitudes of the people walking in the door. It was not about me looking nice or sitting behind a big desk. It was about how people were received and treated, and what that said about who they were and why they mattered: 'You're a person, not a number or a case. You are the king or queen, I am the servant. This is what Native people deserve.' I was not in a position to do that across the organization, but I could change my little piece of it."

Leaders who aspire to do great things can't lose sight of the small things that make such a huge impression inside and outside the organization.

It's a long way from a fresh coat of paint and an oak desk to a MacArthur genius grant and a Baldrige Award, but Gottlieb's human-centered instincts have shaped every step of SCF's transformation. For example, one of Nuka System's signature innovations is the "integrated-care teams" through which it delivers basic medical services. Each of these teams, made up of eight different people, treat between 1,200 and 1,400 customer-owners. There's a physician, of course, along with a case manager (always a registered nurse), a dietitian, a certified medical assistant, an administrator, a pharmacist, and a behavioral health consultant (a BHC or behaviorist, for short). Each of these practitioners is encouraged to "work to the top of their license"—that is, to take on as much responsibility as they are legally allowed to, freeing up their colleagues to raise their game and take on more responsibilities as well.

"Our medical assistants are doing what RNs used to do," says Douglas Eby, SCF's vice president for medical services. "Our RNs are doing what primary-care providers used to do. Our primary-care providers are doing what specialists used to do. No one is really trained to work in our system. We basically have to retrain everyone. We've reinvented roles and given people much bigger and more complex responsibilities."

One important virtue of the team-based model is that, with training, it allows for consistent care over time, with plenty of personal attention and seamless communication. Families see the same doctors, nurses, and medical assistants year after year, and these caregivers work together on the same cases, which cuts down on mixed signals, crossed wires, and bureaucratic snafus—all-too-familiar problems in far too many health-care systems. In addition, the low-key, right-from-the-start participation of behaviorists allows for exams to be more conversational and less clinical than in most systems, and creates opportunities for these specially trained counselors, therapists, and social workers to look for warning signs that can fall outside the realm of traditional doctor's visits. They intervene with issues of sleep or stress, advise people on how to adhere to the medications prescribed by their physicians, and help with diet and hygiene. "Doctors are great for diagnosing illnesses and prescribing pills," explains Eby. "But motivating, encouraging, and inspiring people to live healthier lives is better done by other people."

In particular, he says, by SCF's behaviorists. "This role is sort of our invention," he explains. "They can do interventions and referrals on major issues. But they are also the mental-health equivalent of the local hairdresser or the neighborhood bartender—a sounding board, a sympathetic ear, someone you can talk to about what's happening in your life. For the first time I've seen anywhere, we have a delivery system for mental-health services that can reach tens of thousands of people at scale."

That delivery system doesn't begin and end with the integrated-care teams. SCF's leaders are always searching for ways to "meet people where they are in terms of mental and behavioral health," in the words of Chanda Aloysius, vice president of behavioral services. One unorthodox resource, she says, is the dental staff, which is one of the most popular groups at SCF. Dentistry was one of the very first services the foundation provided to the Native population, going all the way back to Katherine Gottlieb's days as a receptionist, so the practice is held in especially high regard. This long-standing emotional connection creates a valuable window into the lives of customer-owners, far beyond cavities or gum disease.

"The dental assistants here are amazing," Aloysius says, "they are so warm, friendly, cheerful." The relaxed atmosphere often gets people to open up and share secrets: "I don't have food in my refrigerator, I'm worried my child may be on drugs, my spouse is beating me up." So a trip to the dentist becomes something else entirely. "In fact," Aloysius says, "we get so many social-service stories in dental that we have a protocol in times of crisis: 'I'm not really here for a toothache, I need to get away from my husband.' We take them out the back, get them into behavioral health, and notify the authorities. When it comes to mental health, every door is the right door."

This emphasis on engaging customer-owners in the fullness of their lives, on making sure that each encounter with a doctor, a pharmacist, or even a dental hygienist is responsive to one-of-a-kind personal struggles and complex family situations, is what makes SCF so effective at what it does. Katherine Gottlieb and her colleagues don't define their work around traditional medical specialties or established professional boundaries, and they don't address chronic health problems (infant mortality, heart disease, obesity) with short-term interventions or one-time programs. Their strategy is built around emotion, empathy, and the slow but steady elevation of personal responsibility and self-esteem among the people they serve.

For example, when I asked Douglas Eby about SCF's noteworthy progress against diabetes, and whether the system had mounted a full-court press to fight the disease, he shook his head and offered a corrective. "The long-term strategy for diabetes is about diet, exercise, sleep, managing stress," he explained. "There's no 'magic pill' for that. People have to be internally motivated to change. So when we're talking to, say, fifty-year-old Alaska Native men, we know that 90 percent of them have or will have grandchildren. That means they are going to want to teach them to hunt and fish, to take them back to the land. So we explain how diabetes hurts your eyesight, how it makes the tips of your fingers feel strange."

Most patients don't respond to white papers, reams of data, and articles from the *New England Journal of Medicine*. "This isn't about statistics," Eby says. "It's about whether grandparents will be able to teach their grandchildren what they want to teach them. There is no aha moment, no stand-alone diabetes-reduction program. It is about the art of influence, adapting to people on their own terms. In our system, you have the capacity to really understand someone's story over time and get them to health."

There is at least one SCF program, it should be noted, that does strive for aha moments and is built around extraordinary interventions. It is also one of the few programs that reports directly to the CEO. Katherine Gottlieb created the Family Wellness Warriors Initiative (FWWI) to address one of the most tragic consequences of the historical mistreatment of Alaska Native people—an epidemic of domestic violence, child sexual abuse, and child neglect that has ravaged families and villages for generations. This was one health challenge, she concluded, that demanded a one-of-a-kind response. The problem was too big, the costs too great, the implications of unspoken historical traumas too vast not to give it special status.

The most intense element of FWWI is an experience called Beauty for Ashes. It is a retreat in which people who have been harmed, as well as those who have committed harm, spend five days and four nights, as many as fourteen hours per day, telling their stories in learning circles, retracing their histories, and coming to terms with what they've done or what's been done to them. Gottlieb, who often leads the sessions herself, calls it "going to ground zero"—a grueling, exhausting, and (hopefully) liberating process of reckoning with past trauma and hidden shame. It is a tough model to scale, different from controlling diabetes or boosting immunization rates. But domestic violence has been so intractable, rooted in centuries of oppression and degradation, that the only program with a chance of success is one that digs deeply (and painfully) into the past of each victim or perpetrator and summons the best of traditional values to move forward. "We are breaking the silence about domestic violence and child abuse," Gottlieb says. "Sometimes we can do in five days what it might take years to achieve."

As the Family Wellness Warriors Initiative has gained more and more traction (as well as outside attention), SCF has committed to training counselors, village leaders, and volunteers across Alaska, well beyond its home base in Anchorage, to achieve greater reach and broader impact. The true goal, SCF's leaders say, is not just to make dramatic progress on a long-ignored health crisis, although that is certainly a goal. "We want people to know what true happiness feels like," Chanda Aloysius explains, "to have joy in their life again." That's a pretty compelling definition of success for any intervention—and the ultimate act of kindness for any organization.

"BE PROVOCATIVE ENOUGH TO CHANGE WHAT PEOPLE DO" —BRAND IS CULTURE, CULTURE IS BRAND

It may seem strange that a smile from a cashier or a flight attendant, or a bit of sympathetic advice from a dental hygienist, could matter so much to the person receiving it (or delivering it). But it does, in terms of both creating more meaningful experiences and building more compelling organizations. The most successful companies I know don't just think differently from everyone else, they *care more than* everyone else. Whether you're building a love-mark or just spreading some love, you can't be exceptional in the marketplace unless you create something exceptional in the workplace. Your brand is the outward expression of your culture, your culture is the platform that sustains your brand.

No organization brings this connection to life more vividly than USAA, the financial-services juggernaut based in San Antonio, Texas. USAA has become an iconic brand with more than 11 million members, roughly 28,000 employees, annual revenues of more than $20 billion, and profits of $2.7 billion. The company, which was formed in 1922 by a group of army officers who agreed to insure one another's cars (the insurance industry decided that military men were a bad risk), has become one of the country's top credit-card issuers, mortgage bankers, and home and auto insurers, as well as, surprisingly, one of its biggest direct banks. With no physical branches, just by engaging customers over the telephone and the Internet, USAA has amassed consumer deposits of roughly $60 billion.

Strategically, what distinguishes USAA as a company is that it still does business almost exclusively with active and retired members of the U.S. military and their families—a big market, to be sure, but one with highly specialized needs. Those are the customers USAA serves, and it serves them absurdly well. ("I consider them to be an industry leader who everyone is chasing," the CEO of a military-oriented financial-services trade association told the *New York Times*.) USAA is legendary for its accessibility, responsiveness, and on-the-spot problem-solving skills. Consult any major survey of customer attitudes and brand loyalty (J.D. Power, Forrester Research) and you'll find it at the top of the list. In 2015, the Temkin Group published its annual "Forgiveness Ratings," which ranks nearly three hundred companies on the willingness of their customers to forgive mistakes, a powerful measure of loyalty and trust. USAA won the top three spots (for its credit cards, banking services, and insurance products), beating glamorous brands such as Apple and Lexus and outpolling financial-services laggards Citibank and Wells Fargo by a factor of three. No other company came close to this performance across multiple product lines.

A big reason for USAA's extraordinary presence in the marketplace, I'm convinced, is its deeply felt sense of connection and conviction in the workplace. The company has a much-admired training program in which frontline employees learn the technical skills they need to work effectively, from the terms and conditions of its mortgages and insurance policies to the best ways to interact with customers via text messages and online chats. But what they really learn is a sense of empathy and a spirit of generosity—to see the world through the eyes of a soldier in Afghanistan who needs to transfer money to a parent, or the spouse of a soldier in Munich who needs to insure a new car for her family in Maine, and to do whatever it takes to make those members happy.

"There is nobody on this earth who understands their customer better than USAA," one researcher told *Bloomberg Businessweek* for its report on "Customer Service Champs" (which ranked USAA at the top). That's because, according to *Businessweek*, "In almost everything it does, the financial-services outfit puts itself in the spit-shined shoes of its often highly mobile customers, many of whom face unique financial challenges."[2]

You can't be exceptional in the marketplace unless you create something exceptional in the workplace.

How do frontline employees put themselves in their customers' spit-shined shoes, or, perhaps more commonly, their dusty boots? They go through a simulated overseas deployment to understand the trials and tribulations of being sent away for a year or more. They eat so-called MREs (Meals Ready to Eat) to get a taste for life in the field. They try on military backpacks and Kevlar vests, the better to appreciate the physical burdens soldiers carry with them every day. They read letters from soldiers to their families, and letters from families to their soldiers. Hundreds of employees even volunteer to sweat and grunt through a version of the Zero Day PT experience of basic training, in which raw recruits face their first encounters with drill sergeants who bark orders, make them do push-ups, and otherwise remind them that they're in the army now. "This was probably the most humbling experience I've ever had," one ten-year USAA veteran told a San Antonio television station after she survived Zero Day PT.

In other words, USAA immerses its employees, managers, and executives in the complex lives and emotional needs of the people they serve, so that everyone understands the level of connection to which the company aspires. This immersion certainly helps colleagues identify with their customers, which fuels and sustains so many stories of legendary service. But it also helps them identify with one another, to develop peer-to-peer bonds that energize their performance.

In many respects, USAA is a conservative, buttoned-down culture. Its CEO is always a retired military leader, and 25 percent of its workforce are veterans or military spouses. So there's a natural respect for order, process, the chain of command. At the same time, when it comes to above-and-beyond feats of customer service and first-in-the-world innovations (allowing members to deposit checks by iPhone, say, or transfer funds via text message), USAA is one of the most nimble, creative, open-minded organizations I've seen. Who has time for politics, bureaucracy, and second-guessing when soldiers, veterans, and their families are depending on you?

This deeply felt sense of service, a spirit among rank-and-file employees that they've signed up for more than just a job, has been alive in San Antonio from the beginning—a product, no doubt, of USAA's origins as a lifeline for army officers whose needs were being ignored by the insurance-industry establishment. Not every company has such a stirring history, but every company can aspire to the level of connection and compassion that USAA has achieved, as long as it invests the kind of attention, creativity, and commitment that USAA does in how it organizes its workplace and the way colleagues treat one another.

High-tech entrepreneur Ben Horowitz, who has become one of the most influential of Silicon Valley's new generation of venture capitalists, calls this leadership challenge "programming your culture." Horowitz thinks, talks, and writes extensively about culture, but not from the point of Foosball tables, free food, and pet-friendly offices—the surface trappings that get so much attention. Instead, he argues that culture is all about "designing a way of working" that serves three essential purposes: it distinguishes you from competitors; it supports the persistence of critical operating values; and it identifies, promotes, and retains employees who fit the mission. When it comes to culture, he says, the defining challenge for leaders is to "be provocative enough to change what people do every day." In other words, if you want to energize and elevate how your organization competes, energize and elevate how your people behave.[3]

"GIVE PEOPLE PERMISSION TO PERFORM" —WHY COMMON LAW TRUMPS ROMAN LAW

Mercedes-Benz USA is an instructive case in point. It's hard to think of a more respected, more admired, more alluring brand than Mercedes-Benz, whose sedans, roadsters, and SUVs have been synonymous with the market for luxury automobiles for decades. But when Stephen Cannon became president and CEO of

Mercedes-Benz USA in January 2012, he recognized that break-away success was about more than just how smoothly his vehicles drove or how elegantly they were designed. It was about how much the people who sold and serviced the brand cared and how generously they behaved. "Every encounter with the brand," he declared, "must be as extraordinary as the machine itself." And almost every encounter with the brand, he understood, came down to a personal encounter with a human being in a dealership—a receptionist or a salesperson, someone from parts or service—who could act in ways that were memorable, or could act the way most people in most dealerships act. (Remember that Cadillac dealer from chapter 5?)

This was a big insight, and a big change. The Mercedes culture has always been about cutting-edge innovation, world-class performance, and an unshakable commitment to excellence—"The best or nothing," in the immortal words of German auto pioneer Gottlieb Daimler. Historically, though, that promise applied to the meticulous process of designing and building the cars themselves, not to the harder-to-control experience of interacting with living, breathing customers. Cannon understood that if he wanted to influence the behavior of more than 23,000 employees at roughly 370 Mercedes dealerships across the United States, he first had to influence what they believed. There was no rule book he could write, no set of procedures he could prescribe, no systematic way to engineer a culture of connection, commitment, and compassion. Instead, he had to convince his dealers and their frontline staffers to join a grassroots "movement" in which people were "driven to delight" everyone they encountered. Mercedes-Benz, like USAA, had to be more than just a company, it had to become a commitment.

"There is no scientific process, no algorithm, to inspire a sales-person or a service person to do something extraordinary," Cannon tells me during an in-depth conversation about his far-reaching initiatives. "The only way you get there is to educate people, excite them, *incite* them. Give them permission to rise to the occasion when the occasion to do something arises." How does he give people that permission? "You try to create an ecosystem, a movement, in which people are aware of the opportunities they have to do things customers don't expect, things they don't have to do, but that have real meaning and make a lasting impression. This is not about following instructions. It's about taking a leap of faith."

Cannon sighs when he talks about how rote, by-the-book ef-forts to engage customers can produce robotic, paint-by-numbers behaviors that have little or no effect. "The water bottle!" he ex-claims. "At some point, car dealers decided it would be nice to give customers a bottle of water when they walked into the showroom or the service department. But over time, something that was meant as a thoughtful gesture became a process, and water started arriving from all directions: Here comes a damn water bottle again! When you take a gesture and turn it into a process, it loses its meaning, it almost becomes a mark of failure."

Compare that, he says, with impromptu acts of kindness and connection that customers will appreciate for years. There was one Mercedes dealer who'd closed a sale, was completing the paper-work, and noticed from the financial documents that it was the customer's birthday. So he ordered a cake, and when the customer came in to pick up the car, there was a celebration as well. "It was a complete surprise," Cannon says, smiling, "and the reaction was incredible." Then there was the customer who got a flat tire on the way to her son's graduation. She pulled into a Mercedes dealership in a panic and explained the problem. Unfortunately, there were no replacement tires in stock for the model she was driving. Rather than throw up his hands, the service manager ran to the showroom, jacked up a new car, removed one of its tires, and sent the mother on her way in time for the ceremony.

"We have so many stories like this," Cannon says. "They're about people making the right call on the spot, going out of their way, because they care enough to do something special." Cannon and his colleagues made it a point to collect these sorts of stories, capture them on video, and then share them across the company's dealerships in order to help frontline employees visualize success, to give them, in his words, "snapshots of the future" they aimed to create.

"The good news is that the future already exists, in pockets and episodes," he explains. "We're not chasing the impossible. These stories also humanize our customers. They're not just names behind satisfaction scores, they are real live human beings. And a big part of what we can do is to make their lives a little easier."

Lior Arussy, the strategist and consultant we heard from earlier, worked closely with Cannon and his team on their grassroots movement inside Mercedes-Benz USA. He offers a more universal twist on the president's insights and stories. "Remember, your employees are customers of lots of other companies," he told me. "They know how they like to be treated. If we can unleash those instincts, if we can liberate their energies and emotions, they will surprise us with their compassion and creativity. We don't need to script everything in advance for people to behave in memorable ways. We just need to give them permission to perform."

Mark White, a business theorist who studies what he calls

"adaptive organizations," makes an intriguing distinction between companies that are based on Roman law principles of governance and decision making and those based on common law principles. In Roman law, White explains, anything that is not expressly permitted is forbidden. So Roman law companies rely on formal policies and bureaucratic procedures, predetermined rules and established practices. In common law, anything that is not expressly forbidden is permitted. So common law organizations rely on fast action, nimble reactions, good judgment, and common sense. Needless to say, when it comes to growth, innovation, and the capacity to change with the times, common law organizations trump Roman law organizations, even though the biggest, most established companies remain stuck in the Roman law mind-set. Rome may not have been built in a day, but the days of Roman law organizations dominating the landscape are numbered.

> **Most companies run under Roman law: Anything not expressly permitted is forbidden. The most human companies run under common law: Anything not expressly forbidden is permitted.**

Harry Hynekamp, a fifteen-year veteran of Mercedes-Benz USA, was named the first-ever general manager for customer experience a few months after Steve Cannon became CEO. He doesn't spend lots of time thinking about the distinction between Roman law and common law, but he does reflect on the best ways to build the kind of grassroots spirit of empathy and execution that allows organizations such as Southcentral Foundation and USAA to connect so well with so many people. One part of the process, he agrees with Steve Cannon, is to "humanize the customer" to frontline employees. But just as important, he adds, is to build pride in the brand and a more powerful sense of affiliation within the organization. People are more likely to do extraordinary things for customers, he argues, when they have an extraordinary sense of connection to the company and their colleagues.

That was the thinking behind a program called DaSH, for Drive a Star Home. (The three-pointed star is the universally recognized trademark of Mercedes-Benz.) As Hynekamp and his team traveled across the country and interacted with employees from every nook and cranny of the Mercedes network, they discovered, much to their surprise, that "pride in the brand was not quite as strong as we thought, the level of engagement with the work not as deep as we thought," he explains.

What really shocked them, he says, is that nearly 70 percent of frontline employees had never driven one of the cars outside the dealership lot! They'd repaired them, they'd ordered parts for them, they'd displayed them in the showroom, but they'd never really been behind the wheel of one on the open road. How could people take genuine pride in the brand, Hynekamp wondered, why would they be inspired to swap stories, share tips, celebrate a purchase with customers, if they'd never experienced the thrill of driving a sedan, roadster, or other Mercedes-Benz vehicle?

With DaSH, all 23,000 dealership employees got the opportunity to experience a new Mercedes-Benz as they saw fit for forty-eight hours. The company put close to 800 cars in the field, at a cost of millions of dollars. They briefed participants about the models they'd be driving, and got feedback later on how the vehicles performed and what they learned. But the power of the experience wasn't about features, functions, gizmos, or gadgets. It was about emotion, identity, passion, and pride. Time and again, employees timed their DaSH experience to correspond with important events in their lives—picking up Grandma on her ninetieth birthday, driving a daughter and her friends to a sweet sixteen, bringing a newborn baby home from the hospital. The participants took photos, made videos, and, in one case, even wrote a rap song to chronicle his forty-eight hours.

"The reactions were out of this world," says Hynekamp, who created an internal Web site to collect and share the stories. "Sure, people got to know the cars very well, and we got a benefit because they could use their newfound knowledge and skills with customers—'Let me tell you what happened when I paired up my phone, let me show you this cool feature with the navigation system.' But the biggest piece was the pride piece."[4]

DaSH was a one-time program that made a big-time impression on the thousands of people who participated. Since then, the leadership of Mercedes-Benz USA has taken more steps to deepen the sense of affiliation between frontline employees and the brand, and thus create the conditions for unscripted acts of connection and compassion that deepen the sense of affiliation with customers. Most recently, Mercedes-Benz USA built a Brand Immersion Center at its manufacturing complex near Birmingham, Alabama. The fast-growing plant certainly lives up to the "best or nothing" philosophy of Gottlieb Daimler. It turns out 300,000 cars per year (up from 185,000 in 2013) and can build five different models, from the two-door C-Class coupe to the huge GL-Class SUV. The Brand Center is a combination museum, classroom, and live experience, designed to immerse visitors in the history, design methodologies, and engineering practices behind the cars.

Those visitors, it turns out, will be many of the same people who participated in DaSH originally—thousands of salespeople, department heads, valets, service technicians, and parts managers. They'll spend two days and three nights touring the factory, unpacking the technology, once again driving the cars—this time, both on a track as well as on the highway. Thousands of Mercedes-Benz ambassadors "will experience the brand, our heritage, and the product on and off the road," explains Hynekamp. "They'll see a world-class production facility live and in operation. This is not about sales, it's about inspiring everyone to become a customer-focused brand ambassador. DaSH was a small start. Brand immersion is that experience on steroids."

Steve Cannon had big hopes for the potential of these programs to inspire lots of small acts of kindness among people across the Mercedes-Benz network. (They already seem to be paying off. In 2014, Mercedes-Benz ranked number one in the "J.D. Power Sales Satisfaction Index Study" of customer satisfaction among luxury auto brands, the first time it led the pack in twenty-four years. In 2015, it ran neck-and-neck with BMW as the best-selling luxury auto brand in the United States, a big advance against its German rival.) "Once folks see the levels of excellence we achieve to produce these cars," he argues, "they'll understand that it's our obligation to create a customer experience on par with that. Everything we do has to reinforce the message and standards we are trying to send.

The minute you raise the bar on the customer experience, every-thing is in play."

That's a critical insight, especially in a world, as Lior Arussy emphasizes, in which products and services that seem remarkable when they first appear can quickly become routine parts of life. "Human beings are the most elusive material there is, but only hu-man beings can consistently go beyond what customers expect," he says. "You design a slick mobile phone, people buy it, and then it's not so amazing anymore. It's a phone. You build a beautiful store, the first time I walk in I'm impressed, but after a few visits I take it for granted. It's a store. If you want to create something ex-citing and compelling, a performance that keeps evolving, the hu-man spirit is the only thing that delivers. Leaders have to ask themselves: Do we want to move product, or do we want to move people?"

PART IV

The Allies You Enlist Matter More Than the Power You Exert

Organizations that make the most dramatic progress are the ones that invite ordinary people to make extraordinary contributions, and whose leaders are as humble as they are hungry.

Chapter 7

SERENDIPITY AS A WAY OF LIFE

"We Prize Collisions Over Convenience"

T ony Hsieh could be forgiven if he spent his days flaunting his celebrity or reveling in his wealth and status. As CEO of Zappos, the online shoe and fashion retailer that he still runs after selling it to Amazon for more than a billion dollars in stock, Hsieh (pronounced *shay*) sits atop one of the most popular and successful consumer brands on the Internet. He also sits atop a pile of money. Zappos, famously headquartered in Las Vegas, is Hsieh's second big score of the digital era. In 1999, he sold his first company, an Internet advertising network called Link Exchange, to Microsoft for $265 million. With nearly three million followers on Twitter, countless satisfied customers for Zappos (the company handles hundreds of thousands of orders per week), and hundreds of millions of dollars in the bank, there's no denying that Tony Hsieh is a big brain who has taken big risks and made big waves in the fields of digital branding, customer service, and management itself, especially with his controversial embrace of "holacracy," an organizational model that eliminates traditional hierarchies and distributes authority through the ranks.

On this particular Tuesday afternoon, though, Hsieh is neither counting his cash nor shaking up Zappos's leadership ranks. Instead, he is pointing to a cluttered wall in a sprawling, twenty-third-floor apartment, explaining the nearly two hundred Post-it notes that reflect the hopes, dreams, and suggestions of the thousands of colleagues, friends, business partners, and curious visitors, like me, who have streamed through the place. The wall is a small glimpse into Hsieh's most unconventional bet yet. The Downtown Project is a $350 million urban-development initiative meant to shape the future of a gritty, long-neglected Las Vegas neighborhood, and, just maybe, to reshape how executives, companies, and even whole communities think about the relationship between top-down leadership and bottom-up creativity.

Hsieh's project is a high-risk, high-profile venture—"the most ambitious experiment in building a twenty-first-century utopian city in the U.S.," according to *Re/code*, the influential Web site founded by Walt Mossberg and Kara Swisher that has been deeply skeptical of Hsieh's venture. *Wired* magazine, which published an in-depth evaluation that was far more supportive, described its animating spirit as "an ethos that combines the idealistic, artistic communalism of Burning Man with the can-do workaholism of 21st-century digital entrepreneurialism."[1]

Actually, the Downtown Project is simpler than all that—and more complicated. It began back in 2012. Zappos was growing so fast and adding so many people that it was bursting out of its headquarters in suburban Henderson, fifteen miles off the Las Vegas

Strip. Hsieh knew he would have to find or build a new headquarters, so he went on a tour of iconic campuses (Nike, Google, Apple, and the like) to get inspired. He was impressed by much of what he saw, but perplexed as well. These temples of creativity buzzed with exciting ideas and interesting characters on the inside, but they were sealed off from the outside, where plenty of other new ideas and talented people existed in abundance. The campuses "were great for employees," Hsieh concluded, but they were "really kind of insular, they didn't integrate with or contribute to the community around them."

What if Zappos could design a new headquarters, he wondered, and surround it with artists, geeks, and entrepreneurs—not Zappos employees, but people who might fuel the company with unpredictable kinds of energy and creativity that could keep it moving forward? Zappos could still have a campus with all the creature comforts, but it would be analogous to NYU's campus in the heart of New York City's Greenwich Village, where, as Hsieh puts it, "you don't really know where one begins and the other ends." Rather than locked doors and airtight security, he wanted porous borders between Zappos and its surroundings, to create "the most community-focused company in the world by being integrated into the fabric of the community." People wouldn't have to be part of Zappos to be part of the environment that made it successful, to contribute to the company's success as allies rather than as employees.

As simple as it sounds, this was a mind-bending insight—a perspective on strategy and creativity that worries less about the loss of trade secrets and proprietary technology and more about the loss of energy and vitality. Saul Kaplan, founder of a strategy-and-creativity outfit called the Business Innovation Factory, argues that the process of making strategy has moved beyond filling three-ring binders with five-year plans. Instead, it's about enabling "random collisions of unusual suspects"—creating the conditions for all sorts of interactions among all sorts of interesting people that produce all sorts of unexpected insights about the future. "The best things happen when people are running into each other and sharing ideas," Hsieh agrees. The best way to make those things happen, he concluded, was to embrace serendipity as a way of leadership and life.

Hence the new headquarters, along with the Downtown Project, which is independent of Zappos, but an essential part of how Hsieh envisions the future of the company. It's difficult, in a few paragraphs or pages, to capture the color, energy, and sense of thinly veiled anarchy that swirls around the Downtown Project. Hsieh's goal is to attract thousands of new residents to, and launch hundreds of new businesses in, the Fremont East neighborhood. That's where Zappos moved after it acquired the aging, retro, about-to-be-vacated Las Vegas City Hall. After a top-to-bottom renovation of the complex, Zappos unveiled its corporate campus in September 2013. (True to Hsieh's flair for the dramatic, the grand opening featured the world's largest-ever ribbon cutting, with fifteen hundred people and a one-mile-long ribbon.)

Long before the new headquarters opened for business, Hsieh had launched his bottom-up campaign to energize the cityscape around it. He spent $200 million assembling a sixty-acre parcel of real estate that included hotels, apartment buildings, bars, and restaurants, hundreds of buildings in all. He earmarked $50 million to fund high-tech start-ups, $50 million for neighborhood joints and local entrepreneurs, and another $50 million for culture and the arts. He built the Downtown Container Park, where refurbished shipping containers get stacked like so many LEGO blocks to create a shared social space and appeal to young families. These corrugated metal containers, once stuffed with electronic gadgets from China or cars from Japan, now house art galleries, bakeries, boutiques, and restaurants that offer everything from tacos and barbecue to fine dining. The Container Park also features an outdoor Treehouse with a thirty-three-foot-long slide, an attraction I chose not to experience (in-person research has its limits).

Beyond the buildings, downtown Las Vegas has a carefully designed social infrastructure and rhythm of collaboration in terms of public events and community gatherings. Every month features Tech Week, where geeks and app developers showcase their technology. Then there's Fashion Week, where designers share ideas about clothes, furniture, Web pages, and the like, and often work together in a shared makerspace called Stitch Factory. VCs, entrepreneurs, and tech geeks who can't relocate to Fremont East are encouraged to "subscribe" to the city; they spend one week per month there and serve as mentors and advisers to local start-ups.

Meanwhile, Hsieh acquired and renovated a venue at the well-known intersection of Fremont Street and Las Vegas Boulevard and christened it the Inspire Theatre. The handsome facility hosts presentations from visiting artists, business leaders, and other luminaries in a kind of rolling series of speeches and seminars. The Learning Village is a less-glitzy venue that hosts training-and-education events for community groups and social entrepreneurs. In the spirit of full-on Las Vegas glitz, the annual Life is Beautiful festival covers eleven city blocks in the downtown area, lasts for three days, attracts more than 100,000 attendees, and features musical acts from Stevie Wonder and Duran Duran to Imagine Dragons and Snoop Dogg.

Making strategy is no longer about filling three-ring binders with five-year plans. It's about enabling "random collisions of unusual suspects."

Tony Hsieh offers a pithy phrase to describe what he is unleashing in downtown Las Vegas—"the city as a start-up," he likes to call the phenomenon. The CEO of one of the young companies headquartered in Fremont East described it more colorfully: "Imagine if Walt Disney ran Silicon Valley but everyone lived on the set of *Cheers*." Actually, Hsieh's thinking has been shaped less by Disney fantasies than by the rigorous analysis of a Harvard professor by the name of Edward Glaeser, whose book *Triumph of the City* celebrates the real-world virtues of the social fabric Hsieh is trying to stitch together in Las Vegas. According to Glaeser, the attributes of urban life that critics bemoan and corporate campuses wall off are what make cities "our greatest invention." They are loud, messy, crowded, and expensive. That's why they're also vibrant, prosperous, and creative.

"Rousseau famously wrote, 'Cities are the abyss of the human species,' but he had things completely backward," Glaeser argues. "Cities enable the collaboration that makes humanity shine most brightly. Because humans learn so much from other humans, we learn more when there are more people around us. Urban density creates a constant flow of new information that comes from others' successes and failures. In a big city, people can choose peers who share their interests, just as Monet and Cézanne found each other in nineteenth-century Paris, or Belushi and Aykroyd found each other in twentieth-century Chicago. Cities make it easier to watch and listen and learn."[2]

Tony Hsieh has added a business twist to Glaeser's economic and social arguments, a leadership insight that explains why he is working so hard to enlist so many allies in and around Zappos's headquarters. "We prize collisions over convenience," he explained in an overview of the strategic logic behind the Downtown Project. "We want to be the coworking and colearning capital of the world. Imagine TED or South by Southwest not as events but as a life-style. We have shifted our thinking from short-term ROI, return on investment, to long-term ROC, return on connectedness, and ROL, return on luck."[3]

Hsieh takes the power of collisions seriously—and literally. If he can attract ten thousand new residents into his sixty-acre neighborhood, he figures, he can create an ecosystem that enables "one hundred thousand collisionable hours per acre per year." One of his favorite exercises is to calculate how "collisionable" he is per-sonally. Hsieh estimates that he is out and about in Fremont East three to four hours per day, seven days a week, for the forty weeks of the year he is not traveling on Zappos business. That's "one thou-sand collisionable hours per year"—all sorts of chances to meet new people, connect people who should meet one another, listen to pitches that deserve support, learn about trends in fashion, software, or Web design, and engage in other "opportunities for serendipitous encounters."

In just a few years, these collisions and encounters have turned into a bunch of new businesses. One day at The Beat, Hsieh's go-to coffee shop in Fremont East, the Zappos CEO collided with an aspiring restaurateur by the name of Natalie Young, who had moved to Las Vegas after waging a battle against alcoholism in her native Colorado. Young had been working in the kitchens of some big casinos, from the MGM Grand to the Hard Rock, but she was feeling discouraged and thinking about moving home. Hsieh asked what would keep her in Vegas. She described her vision of a folksy restaurant that would serve breakfast and lunch to locals. The Downtown Project's small-business fund financed the idea, Natalie opened Eat, and it became one of the busiest restaurants in Fremont East—a community hub where more collisions take place over shrimp and grits, made-to-order beignets, and "killer grilled cheese."

Indeed, Eat was so successful, and Natalie's story so uplifting, that American Express featured her in a TV ad that aired during the 2015 Academy Awards, a spot called "Rock Bottom to Restaurateur." Amex's three other Oscar spots featured Aretha Franklin, Mindy Kaling, and GoPro founder Nick Woodman. "Once a month I have to . . . take a picture because the scenery changes so much," Young told *Wired*. "The changes here are no joke. When people hear me speak they say, 'You drank the Kool-Aid,' and I'm like, 'Yup, and it tastes *real* good.'" (In 2015, Young opened her second downtown restaurant, Chow, with a menu that stretches from Southern fried chicken to Chinese food, targeted to the dinner and late-night crowd.)

Jake Bronstein, a thirtysomething cultural celebrity and fashion entrepreneur, also has lots of collisions in downtown Las Vegas, even though, unlike Tony Hsieh or Natalie Young, he doesn't live there. Bronstein has had one of those only-in-America kinds of careers. In 1997, at the age of eighteen, he was a cast member on the MTV reality show *Road Rules*. He later became an editor at *FHM*, the men's fashion magazine, and went on to start a clothing company, Flint and Tinder, known for its made-in-the-U.S.A. men's underwear and the so-called 10-Year Hoodie. Actually, Flint and Tinder is best known for the Kickstarter campaign through which it launched both product lines, two of the most successful fashion-oriented campaigns in Kickstarter history. (For his underwear line, Bronstein asked for $30,000 and raised $300,000. He raised more than $1 million to finance his hoodies.)

Bronstein's cultural celebrity and business acumen caught the attention of Tony Hsieh, who invested in Flint and Tinder, as did some VC firms. Hsieh first proposed that Bronstein relocate to Las Vegas, which was not feasible given the relationships with suppliers and factories he'd established on the East Coast. So Hsieh suggested that Bronstein "subscribe" to the city instead. The third week of every month is Fashion Week, he explained. Bronstein could spend that week in Fremont East, working on his business and also giving seminars on Kickstarter techniques and clothing trends, holding office hours for entrepreneurs looking for advice on manufacturing strategies and supply chains, hanging out at Stitch Factory, and otherwise engaging with the community. If Bronstein spent twelve weeks in Las Vegas per year, Hsieh figured, and was available twelve hours per day, that adds up to one thousand "collisionable hours per year"—the same as for Hsieh himself.

Bronstein, Hsieh argues, "is actually part of the community even though he doesn't technically live here."

Naturally, not all the collisions among artists, designers, and entrepreneurs in Fremont East have led to positive outcomes. Some promising start-ups that began in or moved to Las Vegas flamed out, as happens with start-ups everywhere. One of the Downtown Project's most high-profile tech companies, an outfit called Romotive that was founded to build minirobots powered by iPhones, moved to the San Francisco Bay Area because it could not find enough local talent to support its growth. (Since its move to the Bay Area, Romotive has renamed itself Stork, and raised venture funds from an array of big-name backers to develop a new generation of unmanned aerial vehicles.) Tragically, Jody Sherman, founder of an ecommerce start-up called ecomom, which moved from Santa Monica to be part of the scene in Fremont East, took his own life after his company, which had raised $12 million, abruptly ran out of cash. "We are always on the brink of making it big or losing everything," one of Sherman's fellow CEOs wrote in a blog post after his death. "I hope that now . . . we can begin an open dialogue about suicide and the pressures founders face."[4]

I don't know what the Downtown Project will look like five or ten years from now, or how much of the artistic and entrepreneurial ferment in Fremont East will rub off on Zappos (and vice versa). I'm not sure Tony Hsieh knows either. Of all the case studies I researched for this book, the many different companies and causes in which I immersed myself, this was by far the most contentious and unabashedly *experimental*. In fact, between the time I visited Hsieh in Las Vegas and began writing, he had moved out of his twenty-third-floor apartment and into a tricked-out Airstream trailer in a new downtown space called the Airstream Living Experiment, populated by a collection of mobile homes and Tumbleweed Tiny Houses. There are fewer creature comforts, Hsieh concedes (although the trailers do come with stainless-steel appliances, Bluetooth sound systems, and two TVs), but an even greater sense of community and connection. "It's a constant experimentation with new ideas," Hsieh told *Las Vegas Weekly*. "The whole point is that there's no master plan."[5]

Which is precisely what makes it so valuable, even if it is controversial. Like any important experiment, the final results with the Downtown Project may wind up being less instructive than the lessons learned as it grows, evolves, and suffers the occasional setback—and on this score, there is no denying the importance of Hsieh's initiative. "The big bet is to get all these different, diverse groups together in a relatively small space," he has explained, and "make sure they have a bias to collaborate." Under those conditions, and with a genuine commitment to connectedness, "the magic will happen on its own."

"MY JOB IS TO SET THE STAGE, NOT PERFORM ON IT" —THE CASE FOR HERE-AND-NOW HUMILITY

If there's one lesson at the core of the many different organizations we've encountered thus far, it's that exceptional performance begins with extraordinary insights. Put simply, the organizations with the most impressive results are the ones driven by the most original ideas.

In a few of these organizations, there's no question about who comes up with those ideas and who's responsible for turning them into smooth-running businesses. Vernon Hill's unique take on customer service has been the guiding force behind Metro Bank, and his obsession with detail keeps the culture tight as the company grows. Likewise, it's hard to imagine something as original and arresting as 1111 Lincoln Road without the distinctive imprint of Robert Wennett, who is the signature voice behind the property—so much so that he lives there.

But this big-brained, gimlet-eyed approach to leadership, as effective as it occasionally can be, feels inherently limited. Sure, there will always be a place for larger-than-life CEOs and inspired creative geniuses, from Henry Ford to Steve Jobs to Elon Musk. But for leaders in most organizations, the opportunities are too vast, the problems too vexing, for even the most talented executives to identify and solve on their own. Going forward, the leaders with the biggest impact will be the ones who figure out how to enlist the most allies, not the ones who issue the most commands or exert the most power. In businesses (and social movements) built on ideas, responsibility for generating and evaluating ideas has to become everybody's business.

Think about how a MacArthur "genius" like Rosanne Haggerty reinvented her top-down, big-budget approach to fighting homelessness and came to rely on the energy and savvy of grassroots activists across the country who saw ways to achieve results that she could not have seen on her own. "Our job," she says, "was to find the 'positive deviants' who were doing things differently and ask what we could learn from them." Or how Liisa Joronen created a thriving service business built on frontline decision making, a company in which rank-and-file employees could "use their brains as well as their hands" in an effort to "kill routine before it kills you."

Linda Hill, the Harvard Business School leadership guru who distinguishes between opportunity gaps and performance gaps, has studied how the best executives help their organizations do the most creative work. To that end, she advises the leaders she teaches to change their minds about how they define their jobs and the logic of leadership itself. "Society's notion of the brilliant innovator, the solitary genius with a sudden flash of creative insight, is hard to shake," she is the first to admit. "Those in positions of authority have been taught to think that it's their job to come up with the big idea." In reality, though, "sustained innovation comes when everyone has an opportunity to demonstrate a 'slice of genius'"—small pieces of a larger creative puzzle that emerge over time.

"Breakthroughs come when seemingly ordinary people make extraordinary contributions," Hill argues. "If you want your team to produce something truly original, you don't know where you're going, almost by definition. The traditional leadership model just doesn't work." In her book *Collective Genius* (written, appropriately enough, with three coauthors), Hill offers the outlines of a new mind-set. "Instead of trying to come up with a vision and make innovation happen themselves," she writes, "a leader of innovation creates a place—a context, an environment—where people are willing and able to do the hard work that innovative problem solving requires." Or, as one CEO described his role, a description Hill and her coauthors endorsed: "My job is to set the stage, not perform on it."[6]

In businesses (and social movements) built on ideas, responsibility for generating and evaluating ideas has to become everybody's business.

I got an early glimpse of this emerging leadership style more than a dozen years ago, during the first Internet boom, when I met a soft-spoken Canadian gold miner by the name of Rob McEwen. At the time, I was editing *Fast Company* and McEwen was running a company called Goldcorp, which had acquired a troubled property in Ontario's Red Lake district, some 1,300 miles northwest of his company's Toronto headquarters. The Red Lake mine was an economic basket case, notorious for low productivity and bitter labor strife. But it also showed intriguing signs of promise. McEwen's geologists had detected deposits of gold vastly richer than anything found on the property before. But how big were the deposits? And where on the 55,000-acre site should they make the expensive transition from exploratory drilling to deep drilling for volume production? Those questions would make or break Goldcorp. McEwen's strategy for answering them led to an unprecedented strategic breakthrough, an initiative so far ahead of its time that it looks advanced even today.

How did the CEO approach his bet-the-company moment?

Rather than hire a few more technical specialists to crunch data, or hunker down in a command center with digital maps and soil samples, he invited the whole world to advise him on where he should drill. Drawing inspiration from the come-one-come-all creative ethos of open-source software, he posted fifty years' worth of geological data about his mine on the Web, along with software to display the data for anyone who wanted to analyze it. He created a pool of prize money ($500,000 in all) and assembled a blue-ribbon panel of judges to evaluate the ideas the company received and award money to the best proposals. Beyond monetary rewards, he celebrated the geologists and engineers who submitted the most creative plans for where his company should drill, inviting them to attend a major gold-mining conference and show off their talents to his CEO peers. Basically, he turned a bunch of unknown brainiacs into minicelebrities in the gold-mining business. These brainiacs were eager to become his allies, to contribute to his success and the success of his company, because he was willing to contribute to their success both financially and professionally.

McEwen called his initiative the Goldcorp Challenge, and it took the mining field by storm. More than 1,400 "online prospectors" from 50 countries downloaded the data, and more than 140 individuals or teams submitted detailed drilling plans. The plans were so ingenious, the insights so above and beyond what McEwen's team had generated on its own, that they turbocharged the mine and transformed the company. Red Lake became one of the most productive gold mines on the planet, with more than 6.6 million ounces of low-cost ore available for production. And Goldcorp, thanks to the prodigious output of its once-troubled property, along with a series of savvy acquisitions, became one of the world's most valuable mining companies, with a share price that increased a head-spinning thir-tyfold in just twelve years, outperforming such big-name stocks as Microsoft and Berkshire Hathaway over that same period.[7]

Ultimately, the most important lesson of the Goldcorp Chal-lenge was not about the power of technology. It was about the vir-tues of *humility*. As a CEO, McEwen was honest enough to admit that he and his senior team did not have the wherewithal to gener-ate the ideas they needed to seize a huge, career-defining opportu-nity. The gold mine McEwen controlled became valuable only when he unleashed the genius of scientists and engineers who did not work for him but were eager to work with him, because, in the spirit of Linda Hill's CEO, he created a stage on which they could perform.

Edgar Schein, professor emeritus at the MIT Sloan School of Management and a renowned expert on leadership and culture, has spent decades studying the attributes that define great executives. One of the attributes he highlights time and again is humility of a very particular sort. In a lovely book called *Humble Inquiry*, in which he explores "the gentle art of asking instead of telling," Schein iden-tifies three different forms of humility. The first, "the humility that we feel around elders and dignitaries," is a basic part of social life. The second, "the humility that we feel in the presence of those who awe us with their achievements," is a standard part of professional life. It's the third form of humility, which he calls "here-and-now humility," that is the one most rarely observed in business, and the one most relevant for leaders who want to achieve big things.

What is here-and-now humility? It's "how I feel when I am de-pendent on you," Schein explains. "My status is inferior to yours at this moment because you know something or can do something that I need in order to accomplish some task or goal. . . . I have to be humble because I am temporarily dependent on you. [But] I also have a choice. I can either not commit to tasks that make me dependent on others, or I can deny the dependency, avoid feeling humble, fail to get what I need, and, thereby, fail to accomplish the task or unwittingly sabotage it. Unfortunately people often would rather fail than to admit their dependence on someone else."[8]

Why would leaders be willing to fail rather than embrace a spirit of here-and-now humility that could help them succeed? Because in a culture of "gamesmanship" and "one-upmanship," executives "take it for granted that telling is more valued than asking," Schein argues. "To ask is to reveal ignorance and weakness. Knowing things is highly valued, and telling people what we know is almost automatic because we have made it habitual in most situations." Schein once asked a group of students what it meant to be promoted to the rank of manager. "They said without hesitation, 'It means I can now tell others what to do.'" Of course, he warns, "the dangerous and hidden assumption in that dictum is that once people are promoted they will then know what to do. The idea that the manager might come to a subordinate and ask, 'What should we do?' would be considered abdication, failure to fulfill your role. If you are a manager, or a leader, you are supposed to know what to do, or at least appear to know."

Schein's call for a new style of leadership feels so liberating because it provides such welcome relief from the know-it-all ethos that has defined leadership for so long. "Deep down many of us believe that if you are not winning, you are losing," he writes. The "tacit assumption" among executives "is that life is fundamentally and always a competition. . . . The idea of reciprocal cooperation where both parties win is not on our radar screen." Schein wants executives to put that idea on their radar screens. Humility and ambition, he argues, need not be at odds with each other. Instead, humility *in the service of ambition* is the most effective and sustainable mind-set for leaders who aspire to do big things in a world filled with huge unknowns.

Gary Hamel, one of the most influential management thinkers of the last twenty-five years, argues that going forward, the new outlook pioneered by executives such as Tony Hsieh and Rob McEwen will become the rule rather than the exception, and will reshape the very logic of how organizations work. That's especially true for companies that want to stay relevant to what Hamel calls "Generation F"—engineers, finance types, and other key contributors raised on the peer-to-peer connectivity of Facebook. Leaders who aspire to build their organizations around exceptional ideas, he says, have to embrace the new logic of where ideas come from in every aspect of how their organizations operate. These "postbureaucratic realities," built around the "social milieu" of the Web rather than the "legacy management practices" that define most companies, will determine how attractive organizations and their leaders are to prospective employees and outside partners, and whether executives are thought of as "with it" or "past it."

Humility and ambition need not be at odds. In fact, humility *in the service of ambition* is the most effective mind-set for leaders who aspire to do big things in a world with huge unknowns.

What are some of the essential qualities of postbureaucratic organizations and their leaders? For one thing, Hamel argues, *all ideas compete on an open footing*: "Ideas gain traction based on their perceived merits, rather than on the political power of their proponents." What's more, *contribution counts for more than credentials*: "Position, title, and academic degrees—none of the usual status differentiators carry much weight." Importantly, *resources get attracted, not allocated*: "Human effort flows toward ideas and projects that are attractive (and fun) and away from those that aren't." As for senior executives, *leaders serve rather than preside*: "Credible arguments, demonstrated expertise, and selfless behavior are the only levers for getting things done." And, perhaps most tellingly, *power comes from sharing, not hoarding*: "To gain influence and status, you have to give away your expertise and content." On the Web, Hamel continues, "No one can kill a good idea," "Everyone can pitch in," "You get to choose your cause," "Excellence usually wins (and mediocrity doesn't)," and "Great contributors get recognized and celebrated." The challenge for leaders, he concludes, is to create organizations that reflect these same principles.[9]

"YOU DON'T GET TO DEFINE US, WE DEFINE OURSELVES" —NEW-WAVE LEADERSHIP IN AN OLD-SCHOOL ORGANIZATION

I don't mean to suggest that a new style of leadership, based on a spirit of "here-and-now humility" and a respect for the creative virtues of "random collisions of unusual suspects," requires an entirely new leadership style—entrepreneurs with the eccentricities of ecommerce titan Tony Hsieh, the convention-busting vision of mining innovator Rob McEwen, or the informal, peer-to-peer sensibilities of app developers steeped in the work styles of the Facebook crowd. A commitment to embracing the power of collective genius, to recognizing that what you unleash matters more than what you control, can reshape the logic of leadership and success in organizations with all sorts of histories and cultures, and among executives and company builders with many different personal styles. You don't need to live an unconventional life, or be a card-carrying member of Generation F, to appreciate that the best ideas can come from the most unexpected places—and that the leaders who do the best job of attracting those ideas are the ones who generate the most impressive results.

As an instructive case in point, consider the remarkable long-term performance of a little-known company called Fastenal, based in the quiet town of Winona, Minnesota (population twenty-eight thousand). A few years back, when *Bloomberg Businessweek* went in search of the single best-performing stock in the United States in the twenty-five years following the Black Monday crash of October 1987, its journey didn't end at the Apple campus in Silicon Valley, or at Microsoft headquarters in Redmond, Washington, or at Berkshire Hathaway's offices in Omaha, Nebraska. It ended at Fastenal headquarters in Minnesota's bluff country on the banks of the Mississippi River, a two-hour drive southeast from the Twin Cities, a four-hour drive northwest from Milwaukee. (Besides being home to Fastenal, and being considered the unofficial "Stained-Glass Capital of America," Winona's biggest claim to fame may be the actress Winona Ryder, who was born in nearby Olmsted County but named after the town.)

In what glamorous, high-margin, cutting-edge field has this hyperperformer made its mark? Software? Biotech? Aerospace? Not exactly. Fastenal is one of the country's biggest and most important distributor of industrial supplies (nuts and bolts, along with cutting tools, safety equipment, lighting, and all sorts of specialty parts) for factories, mills, construction sites, and other facilities. In other words, if you're a big construction company, a small contractor, an oil driller, or an automobile factory desperate for an exotic bolt or specialty fitting to finish a job or keep a machine running, Fastenal is where you'll find it. And if your part is no longer around or you need something that just doesn't exist, Fastenal will make it for you. It has eleven factories worldwide that can manufacture anything, from fasteners to specialty parts for Arctic energy exploration, mining, and manufacturing, for all kinds of technically demanding endeavors. As the company likes to say about its factories, "We make the unavailable part available."

Fastenal may be pretty invisible in the public imagination, but it is indispensable in the lives of its customers. It is also huge. The company employs thousands of people who work in nearly 2,700 stores, with locations that stretch from the country's biggest cities and industrial centers to rural communities even smaller and more remote than Winona. Its online catalog offers hundreds of thousands of different items. It also has installed more than 60,000 "fully customized and automated Fastenal stores" at factories, warehouses, construction sites—basically, high-tech vending machines for cutting tools, safety gear, and all sorts of other industrial supplies and equipment. It is, in short, a distribution powerhouse whose presence extends into virtually every nook and cranny of the economy.

The result of this overwhelming reach—a wider variety of products offered through more channels at a greater number of physical and virtual locations than any other company in the industry—is truly overwhelming business performance. According to *Bloomberg Businessweek*, Fastenal shares rose 38,565 percent in the quarter century after Black Monday. Microsoft, by contrast, was up 10,000 percent (still not too shabby), and Apple was up 5,542 percent. No stock goes straight up, of course, and in the last few years, with major slowdowns in the worldwide construction market and sharp price meltdowns in the energy sector, Fastenal shares have been under pressure. Still, an investor who bought and held $10,000 worth of Fastenal stock in October 1987 would have had *$3 million* by October 2015. And the company itself just keeps getting bigger and bigger. At the time of its IPO in August 1987, Fastenal had 250 employees and $20 million of revenue. By 2015, it had more than 18,500 employees and $3.7 billion in revenue.[10]

There's a vital lesson behind such high-flying results in such a low-key field, a lesson that drives home the central message of this chapter. I got that message loud and clear when I traveled to Winona, Minnesota, to make sense of the Fastenal story. My first in-depth session was with Lee Hein and Gary Polipnick, top executives who traveled well-worn paths at the company. Both started in the mid-1980s, before the IPO, when Fastenal was all of fifty people working in a handful of stores. Both moved from store to store, region to region, and finally into senior leadership. Polipnick became executive vice president of FAST Solutions, the company's ecommerce arm, in January 2016, and Hein has served in a range of leadership positions, most recently as senior executive vice president of sales.

What's the most important part of Fastenal's success that out-siders like me, discovering the company for the first time, don't un-derstand? "The number one thing for me is the people aspect," Hein replied. "The goal is to unleash entrepreneurial passion, a commit-ment that I will be self-driven to do better than what you can ex-pect. It's a mind-set: Run your business like you own it. When you trust people to solve problems and make decisions, and then let them go, that's when the magic happens. That is the story of this company."

In other words, the energy and drive that Fastenal unleashes among its frontline people matter just as much as the ware-houses and distribution assets it controls. To be sure, the company exudes an aura of power and muscle. It is a national (and global) distributor. It also manufactures more and more products on its own, and sells these super-specialized (and often high-margin) items to some of the world's most demanding customers. At the same time, Fastenal embraces a spirit of radical decentralization and autonomy. Each of its twenty-seven hundred stores operates as a stand-alone business, with a clear leader, full P&L (profit and loss) responsibility, and grassroots zeal for growth and service. It also maintains a proudly old-fashioned culture, a throwback sensi-bility of sorts, that recruits many employees while they're still at-tending college, starts a majority of them in part-time jobs, prizes lifetime careers, and drills everyone on the timeless basics of sales and service.

"We grow from the ground up, based on the actions and deci-sions of thousands of people who run their businesses like they own it, who stay up late thinking about the next customers, the next piece of business," Lee Hein says. "And I want those people to stay with us forever. They will never have to stop at a certain level. You may have to move, you may have to learn a new [market] category, but there will always be opportunities here."

> "Run your business like you own it. When you trust people to solve problems and make decisions, and then let them go, that's when the magic happens."

All told, there is a quietly fierce, and fiercely determined, attitude among the people you meet at Fastenal, a palpable sense of both ambition and humility that Edgar Schein would recognize, and that's different from the brash, disruptive energy in Silicon Valley, or the money-centered, me-first outlook on Wall Street. In fact, Fastenal includes ambition as the first of its four core values, and defines it as a blend of five related attributes. *Aggressive:* "a persistent attitude toward the execution of job-related goals." *Confident:* "being certain of one's abilities." *Energetic:* "a fast-paced enthusiasm toward your job." *Motivated:* "an internal desire to be the best you can." *Self-reliant:* "approaching tasks, or your job, in a determined and independent fashion." These may not be new-wave sensibilities, but they have supported a wave of competitive excellence that is hard to match.

"The toughest thing to understand for the new generation coming in is the culture," says Gary Polipnick. "We want people with common sense, a strong work ethic, people who want to learn the business, understand our customers, figure out how to solve their problems and save them money. We call ourselves a blue-collar sales company. When our folks in the stores are doing it right, customers say, 'This guy knows my business better than I do.' We don't care where you went to school, we care about what they can't teach in school—wisdom, savvy, entrepreneurial spirit."

Actually, Fastenal has created a school of its own to teach the business skills, sales techniques, and service mentality around which its bottom-up culture is built. The Fastenal School of Business was launched in 1999 by Peter Guidinger, a PhD chemist who put together a handful of courses on the basics of sales and service. Today it has 39 instructors, 20 campus locations, and more than 300 different courses, from ten-minute e-learning modules to one-week and two-week programs. (True to form, Fastenal designs and develops all the course material itself.) It even offers introductory courses in welding and metalworking, as a way to help salespeople relate more personally to their manufacturing customers. Nearly 9,000 employees spent time in the classroom in 2014, and the workforce as a whole completed nearly 280,000 online courses. It also publishes a widely read paperback, *The Little Blue Book of Customer Service*, which has become a bible of sorts for parables on how to treat customers.

"There are a lot of people who want to be told what to do," says Peter Guidinger. The curriculum at the Fastenal School of Business reflects "our belief in the potential of people. It encourages decentralized decision making and as much autonomy as possible throughout the company."

This agile, flexible, bottom-up approach to building the culture is what makes Fastenal such an intriguing and refreshing organization to encounter—a company that is as nimble as it is disciplined. It also reflects the strategic mind-set with which Fastenal's leaders have built the business as a whole. Five cofounders, led by Robert Kierlin, Fastenal's first and longest-serving CEO, who remains a living legend in Winona, opened a one-thousand-square-foot store to sell nuts and bolts back in 1967. (That first store is now the company museum.) They waited a full four years to open a second location, in nearby Rochester, home to the world-famous Mayo Clinic. By the time of the IPO in 1987 there were still only fifty stores, all clustered in the upper Midwest. Yet even as the company has emerged as a colossus, and has ventured far afield from fasteners (although they still account for 40 percent of total revenue), it has never used big acquisitions or high-risk maneuvers to jolt the business forward. It expands one location, one product category, one customer, at a time. I may be the cofounder of a magazine called *Fast Company*, but I am struck by how Fastenal's slow, steady, methodical approach to growth has served it so well, especially when it is built on a foundation of rank-and-file autonomy. Like so many of John Doerr's Silicon Valley missionaries, Fastenal runs its business as a marathon, not a sprint.

"Fasteners are the tip of the spear," Lee Hein told me. "We get your fastener business, we do a great job. Then we get your cleaning supplies. So we do more. We say, 'Hey, we can do gloves and safety glasses, cutting tools, welding supplies.' Then people need a bolt they can't find. So we make it for them, and we do more again. When you help someone out by making a part they can't get anywhere else, when you keep a mill running that would have shut down for two days, that's a difference maker. We want to know our customer's business so well—what they spend, how they could be more efficient—they can't imagine doing business with someone else."

Even the one real sprint in the company's history, the game-changing rise of its vending-machine channel, is actually an example of its marathon mind-set. The original "business plan" for Fastenal was sketched on a piece of paper by Bob Kierlin, a sketch now on display at the company museum. That sketch, believe it or not, was for vending machines that Kierlin wanted to place in factories and shops around Winona, to dispense boxes of nuts and bolts as customers needed them. He never could find or develop a machine that worked, so he opened a store instead. Nearly fifty years (and several generations of technology) later, Fastenal does one third of its business with customers that have installed its vending machines. These machines, it's important to note, almost never subtract from the business customers do with the stores. They offer one more way to go deeper and do more, to solve problems and sell products.

Thus explains the agile giant that is Fastenal. It rejects the "either-or" choices that determine strategy and culture at most companies—big or nimble, high tech or high touch, cutting edge or conservative—in favor of a "both-and" mind-set that relies as much on the energy and ingenuity of its people as on the scale of its warehouses and the intelligence of its industrial vending machines. I wish more organizations and leaders could be less obsessed with the resources and assets they control, and more confident about what happens when they set the stage for others to perform.

"You get it!" Lee Hein says, chuckling, as I try to frame the big-picture insight behind the company's performance over the last several decades. "We're not one giant organization. We're twenty-seven hundred small businesses wrapped up into one big company. Society tell us, 'You're a big company, act like it!' We say, 'No! You don't get to define us, we define ourselves.' We go against the grain in almost everything we do."

Chapter 8

NOBODY WINS UNLESS EVERYBODY WINS

"Create More Value Than You Capture"

T he Odney Club in the English village of Cookham, less than thirty minutes north of Windsor Castle, is every bit as quaint and verdant as an American visitor would expect. Lullebrook Manor, an eighteenth-century estate (the original home on the property was built in the thirteenth century), is the heart of the club, with sitting rooms and terraces that summon a spirit of simpler times. Lush green lawns and colorful gardens leave no doubt about the meticulous attention they receive. The River Thames flows gently nearby, home to a noisy flock of swans, which are rounded up, marked, and released during the third week of every July by the Queen's Swan Uppers as part of a five-day ceremony (basically, a swan census) that has gone on for nine hundred years. The Cookham section of the Thames is also known as the backdrop for the children's novel *The Wind in the Willows*, published in 1908, with one of the characters based on a real-life tenant of Lullebrook Manor.

Today, however, amid this rich and colorful history, all eyes at the Odney Club are fixed firmly on the future. Senior executives, middle managers, and frontline staffers from two of Great Britain's best-known brands have gathered to evaluate the performance and prospects of one of the country's most original business organizations. The John Lewis Partnership is a huge and hugely successful enterprise, with annual revenues of more than $15 billion, profits of more than $660 million, and some ninety-four thousand employees in England, Scotland, and Wales. Those employees work at two of Britain's most admired retailers, John Lewis department stores and Waitrose supermarkets, each of which has carved out a powerful bond with customers, and both of which have big plans for growth and change.

The first John Lewis opened in 1864 on London's fashionable Oxford Street, where it now operates an elegant, state-of-the-art flagship store, along with 42 other shops and a fast-growing online presence. (The original Oxford Street shop was destroyed by German bombers during World War II.) Waitrose began in 1904 as a small local grocer in West London, was acquired by John Lewis in 1937, and operates 336 supermarkets and convenience stores with a reputation for high-quality products and high-touch service. In fact, back in 2002, Waitrose became the first supermarket to receive a Royal warrant from Queen Elizabeth to supply groceries, wine, and spirits to the Royal Household, and Prince Charles granted his Royal warrant in 2010—two pretty good endorsements.

What truly distinguishes the John Lewis Partnership, though, what makes it a one-of-a-kind organization in Great Britain (and perhaps the world), is that it is owned 100 percent in trust for its employees. There are no public shareholders clamoring for higher dividends, no hedge funds gorging on management fees, no senior executives with options looking for quick ways to bump the stock price. All ninety-four thousand employees are considered and treated as partners in the business. They share in big year-end bonuses based on the company's financial performance, participate in a generous and well-funded pension plan, and enjoy perks and benefits (including access to a sixteenth-century castle with a private beach in southern England and a lakeside club in north Wales) that most companies would reserve for their top brass.

Make no mistake: John Lewis and Waitrose are bold and aggressive players in their respective marketplaces, known for competitive pricing, big innovations in service and delivery, and booming Internet operations. At the same time, they reject the lowest-common-denominator wage-and-benefit policies that define so much of the retail sector, in favor of a commitment to sharing the wealth they create with everyone who helps to create it. This partnership model has become so financially productive, and so socially appealing, that the government of Prime Minister David Cameron has talked openly about the virtues of building a "John Lewis economy"—a "genuinely inclusive and popular" form of capitalism in which more and more people own a stake in where they work and share in their companies' profits.[1]

Even more noteworthy, the partnership operates as a full-fledged democracy that distributes power, as well as profits, up and down the ranks—a business organization that can feel as much like a country as like a company, where employees and their elected representatives debate issues large and small. Democracy at John Lewis is not a metaphor or a state of mind. It is a system of management and governance that includes access to financial information, the right to express opinions without fear of retribution, and elections to boards and councils that have a say in strategy and monitor performance. Indeed, the organization takes grassroots participation and shared decision making so seriously that it has fifty full-time "democracy coaches" whose only job is to deepen the level of engagement and participation. There's even an independent ombudsman, a senior official called the Partners' Counsellor, whose primary role is to make sure the company stays "true to its principles."

"We treat democracy as a functional part of our business," explains Jane Burgess, who began her career with John Lewis in 1975 and now serves as the high-profile Partners' Counsellor. "In the same way that we support selling partners, so they give better service to customers, democracy coaches support our partners, except the product is democracy. Their role is to make sure that our democracy is as healthy as it can be in the same way that we want customer service or logistics to be as healthy as they can be."

The building block of democracy at John Lewis, its version of municipal government, is PartnerVoice. Every two years, employees at each department store, grocery store, or warehouse (more than four hundred locations) select roughly ten of their peers (so more than four thousand people in all) to represent their facilities. These local bodies gather information and opinions, meet with managers, and express the views of their colleagues on workaday issues. Democracy coaches spend much of their time at this level, teaching members how to run more effective meetings, move conversations toward consensus, and be better advocates with store managers. They also listen for problems and worries that cut across locations and deserve wider attention. "We strive for excellence at the local level," Burgess says, "and we raise the profile of issues that seem to be bubbling up in many places."

Every three years, employees from regional groups of John Lewis or Waitrose stores elect representatives to Forum, the next rung on the democratic ladder (comparable, say, to county government). Elected members of Divisional Councils (think state legislatures) deal with issues that concern all of John Lewis or Waitrose. I traveled to Cookham to observe the Partnership Council, whose sixty-six elected members serve as the full organization's version of Congress, debating and voting on big strategic issues and holding the chairman to account, including a vote, twice a year, on whether he should stay in office. The ultimate governing body is the Partnership Board, essentially a board of directors (the executive branch). Five of the fifteen members of the board are elected by the Partnership Council, so that democratic participation reaches the very top of the organization.

Where there are elections, by the way, there are campaigns. And the higher the level of office, the more the elections resemble polite versions of political campaigns in the United States or the United Kingdom. "If you come into a store or a branch when we're in main elections for Partnership Council," Burgess says, "you'll see posters, people walking around with badges, 'Vote for Me!' The campaigns aren't necessarily issue based, they're more about building trust in the candidates, but there are campaigns." (Voter turnout, the share of employees who take the time to cast a ballot, averages about 70 percent, Jane Burgess reports. By contrast, fewer than 58 percent of eligible voters cast their ballot in the 2012 U.S. presidential election.)

It may sound unwieldy, perhaps downright inefficient, but it's how things have worked since 1929—and they've worked quite well. In fact, it's all set out in writing, in The Constitution of the John Lewis Partnership. The constitution establishes 113 principles that determine how the organization is governed, including a right to "comfortable and businesslike but not luxurious" working conditions, "openness, tolerance, and freedom to express criticism, questions, and suggestions (even at the risk of controversy)," and a responsibility of management to "recognize the importance of a healthy balance between the needs of the Partnership and the personal life of the Partners."[2]

The constitution also dictates when elections take place, the role of in-house "journalism," even a requirement that executives respond within twenty-one days to written questions posed by employees, which can be posed anonymously. Most important, it sets out, in Principle 1, why the organization exists in the first place: "The Partnership's ultimate purpose is the happiness of all its members, through their worthwhile and satisfying employment in a successful business. Because the Partnership is owned in trust for its members, they share the responsibilities of ownership as well as its rewards—profit, knowledge, and power."

The constitution is the creation of John Spedan Lewis (1885–1963), one of England's great business visionaries and the founding father, if you will, of the John Lewis Partnership. Spedan (he went by his middle name) joined his biological father's retail operation at age nineteen, when it was all of two stores in London, the original on Oxford Street and a shop called Peter Jones on King's Road. But father and son had a difficult relationship, and eventually a falling out. Spedan "saw that he, his brother, and his father took as much for themselves as the rest of the other 300 employees at Oxford

Street were paid," archivist Gavin Henderson explained to the *Telegraph* for a retrospective on the company's history. "That was the difference in the wage bill, and he saw that it was unsustainable." Spedan "believed that for a business to grow, everyone, from the post-room boy to the staff on the shop floor, had to have a vested interest in it," the *Telegraph* continued. "John Lewis senior didn't like his son's new working practices, and in 1914 they agreed to disagree."

Spedan sold his shares back to his father, took over as chairman of Peter Jones, and put his ideas into practice in his store. "While his father was taking a hard line" with staffers on Oxford Street, the *Telegraph* recounted, "Spedan Lewis was encouraging his employees to play chess, to develop strategic thinking, and, in 1918, he launched the *Gazette*, an in-house newspaper that allowed employees to question management anonymously—and for their queries to be answered by a manager or director." Peter Jones performed exceptionally well, much better than the Oxford Street location. Spedan Lewis assumed control of the whole company when his father died in 1928, and he created the partnership and wrote the constitution the following year. The rest, as they say, is history.[3]

That history is alive and well on a beautiful October morning in Cookham at a packed meeting of the Partnership Council, which has convened, as it does regularly, to consider everything from big strategic issues (intensifying pressures on grocery-store margins, ongoing efforts to diversify the management ranks) to small irritations voiced by frontline staffers (confusion about employee discounts, questions about whether the company's vacation resorts are as popular as they used to be). At the meeting are the sixty-six elected members I mentioned earlier, along with three council members appointed by the company's chairman, Sir Charlie Mayfield, and all fifteen members of the Partnership Board. The meeting is open to any employees who wish to attend, as well as to invited observers like me. (Among my fellow observers were officials from Britain's Trades Union Congress who wanted a glimpse of business democracy at work, as well as change-management types from the BBC who were working to energize their organization's culture.) The meeting was also live-streamed to company locations across Great Britain, John Lewis's twist on C-SPAN.

Unlike most congressional debates on C-SPAN, however, the discussions in the Partnership Council were vigorous and no-holds-barred. The most hotly contested management issue was whether some of the company's recent offerings in the marketplace, which had been an undeniable hit with customers of John Lewis and Waitrose, had exacted too high a toll in the workplace. Councillors worried about frontline managers in particular, many of whom, they argued, weren't equipped to handle the pressures and demands of leading change. "Partners appreciate the need for change," one councillor said, "but we have to address the balance between maintaining partner satisfaction and running a successful business."

This had been a big topic, it turns out, at the previous council meeting in July, so Sir Charlie Mayfield commissioned a report, which was presented at this session. The report validated many of the worries—the organization's innovation agenda had indeed been ambitious, spans of control had stretched well beyond the twenty-to-one target ratio of employees to frontline managers, there was an "air of impatience" about addressing tensions in the stores, a "restlessness" to fix the problems. There was also an air of impatience, a restlessness to fix the problems, among a few of the delegates themselves. "If you were aware of the issues, why did you wait for council to raise them?" one member asked Chairman Mayfield pointedly. "If you weren't aware of the issues, why weren't you?"

The most intriguing part of the meeting, at least to me, was when it came time for the council to vote on whether to approve or disapprove the performance of the chairman. Sir Charlie Mayfield joined the John Lewis Partnership in 2000 as head of business development, after stints as an executive at SmithKline Beecham and a consultant at McKinsey. (In his youth, he'd been a member of the Scots Guards, attended the Royal Military Academy Sandhurst, and served as a captain in the British Army.) He became chairman in 2007, and has been an effective and popular leader inside the organization and out.

In other words, there was no doubt how the vote would go. But that didn't stop the discussion from getting intense, sometimes downright heated, as a few councillors took tough shots at the chairman and his defenders fired back at the criticisms. "I will be voting against Charlie," declared one delegate after an impassioned speech. "You were talking a lot to the camera," another cracked after his critical colleague sat down. This loud dissenter was joined by four softer-spoken colleagues, a tiny caucus of five *no* votes, but one that was confident enough to air its grievances in ways that would be unthinkable in most businesses. (At the next vote of the Partnership Council, in March 2015, Mayfield won with unanimous approval.) It was a free-spirited interaction that John Spedan Lewis would have endorsed, a genuinely democratic moment of the sort that has kept his creation growing and prospering long after his death.

"I am not asking anyone to feel a certain way," declared David

Jones, the outgoing president of the Partnership Council (whose full-time job is supply-chain director at Waitrose), as he moved the vote to a close. "I applaud your skepticism, it's an example of democracy working well. As a member of the Partnership Council, you can say anything you want."

"CREATE MORE VALUE THAN YOU CAPTURE"
—BEYOND WINNER-TAKE-ALL ECONOMICS

Maybe I'm just nostalgic, but in the last few years, I've often been reminded of a message Bruce Springsteen used to deliver back in the mid-1980s. During the height of the "Born in the U.S.A." craze, when the Gipper dominated politics and the Boss ruled pop culture, Springsteen grew visibly uncomfortable with the contrast between Wall Street excesses that were enriching a small segment of society and the struggles of the everyday characters who populated his songs. So he ended his live shows with an admonition that was easy to miss amid the screams and sweat. "Remember," he'd tell the crowd, "nobody wins unless everybody wins."

Three decades later, this simple message seems more relevant than ever—especially for leaders committed to enlisting as many allies as possible in their quest for innovation and impact. Sure, for as long as there have been free markets there have been tensions between equality and efficiency, creativity and security, growth and justice. But never in contemporary history has the distribution of income, wealth, and opportunities for advancement been as one-sided as it is today. A long-standing social compact built on shared prosperity and upward mobility has given way to what economists call a "winner-take-all society," in which small advantages in skill, market power, and luck turn into huge, persistent disparities in outcomes and well-being.

"Over the last generation, more and more of the rewards of growth have gone to the rich and superrich," write Jacob S. Hacker and Paul Pierson in their influential book *Winner-Take-All Politics*, which examines how government policies have made the inequality phenomenon worse rather than better. "The rest of America, from the poor through the upper middle class, has fallen further and further behind."[4]

Why does this matter for business and leadership? Consider the contours of the winner-take-all society from the perspective of a familiar category of frontline workers—bank tellers. A few years ago, the University of California at Berkeley's Labor Center published an eye-opening report that found that nearly one third of all bank tellers in the United States qualified for public assistance, whether it was food stamps, the earned-income tax credit, Medicaid, or the Children's Health Insurance Program. In New York State, the figure was nearly 40 percent. There are roughly 500,000 bank tellers in the United States, many of whom work in institutions that had a hand in the worst economic collapse since the Great Depression and then received massive infusions of rescue funds. Most of those banks are healthy again, with combined profits in 2013 (the year the report was issued) of $141 billion. Yet the median annual income of their tellers was $24,100 (less than $12 an hour), a figure so low that taxpayers shelled out $900 million to help them make ends meet.[5]

It would be funny if it weren't so (pardon the pun) telling. So it goes with winner-take-all economics, and in plenty of fields beyond banking. Indeed, this unprecedented explosion of inequality has become the most pressing piece of unfinished business for executives everywhere, especially for those who want to promote change by mobilizing allies inside and outside their organizations. How can leaders summon colleagues to rethink what's possible in their markets, to do things that others won't do, if they can't summon a sense that everyone is in it together? How can they embrace a commitment to collective genius, and create an environment, as Linda Hill urges, "where people are willing and able to do the hard work that innovative problem solving requires," if they reserve for themselves a disproportionate share of the rewards from those innovations?

Tim O'Reilly, one of the most influential thought leaders of the Internet era, likes to say that successful companies "create more value than they capture." Put another way: The organizations that inspire the deepest sense of commitment in the ranks, and thus have a chance to make the biggest waves in the market, are the ones whose members receive a fair share of the value they help to create.

How can leaders summon colleagues to rethink what's possible in their fields, to do things that others won't do, if they can't summon a sense that everyone is in it together?

This is an article of faith in Silicon Valley, of course, where start-ups grant stock options up and down the ranks—so much so that starry-eyed tales of young Internet millionaires and wannabes have become a cultural cliché, right down to the hit HBO series *Silicon Valley.* Less than fifteen years after its IPO, for example, Microsoft had created an estimated 10,000 millionaires. Bill Gates may have become one of the wealthiest people in history, but thousands of fortunate colleagues shared in the fortune they helped to create. On the morning after Twitter's IPO, 2,300 employees held options worth a collective $3.8 billion. That was $1.68 million *per person.* And who can forget the story of Bonnie Brown, a down-on-her-luck masseuse who answered an ad from a start-up called Google, was paid in stock options for her services, and retired five years later as a multimillionaire, complete with a foundation that supports Christian ministries around the world?[6]

I don't expect every company to operate like a start-up, turning young engineers (and a few lucky masseuses) into millionaires. But the logic of wealth distribution at Microsoft, Twitter, and Google applies well beyond Silicon Valley or Seattle. Put simply, companies generate more ideas and create more value when more people get a piece of the action and a seat at the table. "A host of studies show that workers at firms where employees have a significant stake tend to be more productive and innovative, to retain staff better and to fire them less readily," notes the *Economist* in an article titled "Turning Workers into Capitalists." But "these findings come with a proviso. The effects often depend on whether the employees' ownership stake also brings a greater say in how the firm is run."[7]

In other words, winner-take-all economics is not just an unsustainable way to organize an economy, it's a bad way to run a company. But what's the alternative? I got my first glimpse of what was possible a decade ago, when I traveled to Green Bay, Wisconsin (a long way, geographically and culturally, from Silicon Valley), to visit a company called KI, an office-furniture maker established in 1941. Richard J. Resch joined the company in 1965 and became CEO in 1983, when it was still a small (annual sales of $45 million), undistinguished manufacturer of low-end products like metal folding chairs. Today, it has three thousand employees, revenues of $800 million, and a well-earned reputation as a supplier of elegantly designed furniture for clients in demanding fields, from higher education to hospitals to cutting-edge technology players including Microsoft, Amazon, and Facebook.

KI's new identity in the marketplace, Resch explained to me, would not have been possible without the transformation of its ownership structure. Several years after he became CEO, he engineered a transfer of equity from a small number of top executives to the workforce as a whole. (He still owns about half the shares.) The transaction turned thousands of managers and frontline employees into full-fledged owners who share personally in the value they help to create. At KI, when the company wins, everybody wins.

And it does win. Outside investment bankers perform an annual appraisal that values KI as if it were a publicly traded company. Back in 1990, a few years after the shift to employee ownership, the appraisal valued the shares at $3.80 each. By the end of 2004, after a long boom in many of KI's target markets, shares were worth $27 apiece. That's a fourteen-year compound annual rate of return of close to 15 percent, impressive for just about any manufacturing business, but especially one as brutally competitive and price sensitive as office furniture. By 2015, even after all the pain and turmoil of the global downturn, which took a particularly harsh toll on the office-furniture business, KI shares were worth $43.50. Meanwhile, the company is expanding into India, China, and other fast-growing markets, all of which bodes well for future appreciation in the share price.[8]

The organizations that inspire the deepest sense of commitment are the ones whose members receive a fair share of the value they help to create.

To be sure, no one is going to confuse a forklift driver at KI with a Microsoft millionaire. But everyone at the company has a financial and psychological stake in how it performs and the value it creates. That's a key point. Plenty of leaders say they want their colleagues to "think like owners" when they make decisions about cost, quality, service, and product development. What Resch understood, and what his company's performance demonstrates, is that the most direct way to promote an ownership mind-set among employees is to turn them into actual owners. He also understood that an equity position becomes even more meaningful when employee-owners are steeped in the operating details of the business, and understand how the short-term decisions they make shape long-term valuation. Resch and his colleagues like to say they are making a transition from a culture of "classic capitalism" to one of "social capitalism"—a sense up and down the ranks that everyone has a piece of the action and is part of a cause that matters.

On the third Thursday of every month, for example, Resch and about forty managers squeeze into a conference room and scrutinize results by region, segment, factory, and other variables. Attendees then share the data with their departments, who share it further down the line. By the end of the process, all the company's marketers, designers, and factory workers know which product lines are behind or ahead of plan, which operations are struggling or thriving, and what they can do to help. (When I caught up with Resch in June 2015, he told me the company had recently held its *five-hundredth* consecutive open-book meeting.)

A few years after I spent time with Dick Resch and his colleagues in Green Bay, I traveled to Avon, Connecticut, twenty minutes west of Hartford, and heard a similar message from the head of a different manufacturer. Cecil Ursprung was CEO of Reflexite Corporation, which had production facilities in Connecticut and Rochester, New York, as well as fourteen sites outside the United States. The company makes the reflective material that gets attached to tractor trailers and police cars, construction cones and roadwork signs. Reflexite may not be a household name, but its products are a ubiquitous part of the modern landscape—stuff that shines, glows, reflects, and otherwise contributes to the safety of people who work and travel after dark.

Ursprung, like Resch, had a hard-driving leadership style (in his case, literally hard-driving, as he races cars as a hobby). At the same time, he was open to feedback and ideas from employees at every level. That's because those employees were so invested in the success of the company—also literally. Once a year, based on the performance of their business unit or production site, workers got shares in an employee stock-ownership plan (ESOP) worth 6 to 18 percent of their salaries. That included sixty workers in a factory in the former East Germany and more than one hundred workers in China. Workers could buy additional shares and options for their personal accounts, and many did. "My bosses are all around me," Ursprung said when I toured the Avon technology center. "Three quarters of the equity of this company is in the hands of people who have a direct impact on the business. We attract people who want to be in business for themselves, just not by themselves."

Importantly, those people got a chance not just to own a piece of the business but also to weigh in on how it was run. They attended town hall meetings to discuss strategic issues, got monthly updates on finances and operating results, and were steeped in the company's performance. "People are at their best when they're in a constant state of mild dissatisfaction, when they're always looking to make things a little better," Ursprung told me. "That's what ownership does. I can tell story after story of people going the extra mile, doing things that people in 'normal' companies would never do. People are eager to make an emotional commitment to a cause, especially if they know there is something in it for them. It's remarkable what happens when people get a chance to share in the wealth they help create."

They did create wealth. Reflexite's ESOP took shape in 1985, with an initial contribution of $150,000. By 1995, those shares were worth $20 million. By 2010, the value had topped $40 million. In 2011, after Ursprung had stepped down as CEO, Reflexite made the difficult choice to sell to a German competitor—in part because of the toll exacted by the economic collapse in 2007, in part because of hard-to-fight consolidation in many of its markets. The good news is that the company sold at a huge premium in a great deal for shareholders. The better news is that rank-and-file employees shared in the windfall, because they *were* the shareholders. "Employees up and down the ladder, inside and outside the United States, got treated just like everyone else," Ursprung explains. "This system of ownership created a kind of social justice when it came to such a financial transaction."[9]

"ALL OF US ARE IN THE SAME GAME" —PERSONAL ACCOUNTABILITY, COLLECTIVE IDENTITY

My visits to Green Bay, Wisconsin, and Avon, Connecticut, offered glimpses of small-scale examples, outside the fever-pitch confines of Silicon Valley, of what could happen when rank-and-file employees get a piece of the action and a seat at the table. But it was not until I made two other visits, to two very different organizations, that I came to appreciate that there could be large-scale alternatives to the winner-take-all ethos that has defined and distorted the economy for so many decades.

The first visit was the time I spent in rural England with the John Lewis Partnership. This is an organization, it's worth remembering, that is a household name in Great Britain, with $15 billion in sales and close to 100,000 employees. And it is built not just on a culture of grassroots participation, or even on a generous stock-ownership plan, but on a written constitution with promises that everyone gets a voice, a vote, and a share of the prosperity they help to create. Those promises serve both to reinforce a sense of here-and-now humility among the organization's senior leaders and to

fuel a sense of ambition and contribution among frontline employees.

The constitution comes to life most vividly each March, when
the partnership announces publicly, and with great fanfare, the
size of the annual bonus that all employees receive. (The total pool
is based on that year's operating profits, and each member gets the
same percentage bonus to their annual salary.) Employees of Waitrose and John Lewis gather at the John Lewis flagship on Oxford
Street, as the store manager counts down to the moment of truth
and a company choir bursts into song. In 2014, the bonus came in
at 11 percent of salary, close to six weeks of additional pay. It was,
truth be told, a disappointing result, dragged down by margin
pressures at Waitrose. (The choir "might not be quite in full voice,"
the *Times* of London warned before the announcement.) The year
before, the bonus came in at a healthier 15 percent (a result celebrated with a spirited rendition of "Walking on Sunshine"), and it's
been as high as 24 percent, or thirteen weeks of additional pay.
Whether the bonus gives rise to jeers or cheers, sighs or songs, everyone understands how it's calculated, what it means for them,
and what it says about the health of the business.[10]

But there's more to the sense of common cause at John Lewis
than the bonus celebration. At the top level, the constitution sets
strict limits on CEO compensation. Here's Principle 63: "The pay of
the highest paid Partner will be no more than 75 times the average
basic pay of non-management Partners, calculated on an hourly basis." In 2014, Sir Charlie Mayfield's salary was 66 times the average
pay of nonmanagement partners—generous, to be sure, but a far cry
from what many other CEOs in his position make. Among publicly

traded companies in the United States, for example, the average CEO makes more than *300 times* what average workers get paid.

At the entry level, John Lewis and Waitrose seem more interested in enhancing the compensation of frontline employees than in offering wages low enough to qualify for public assistance. On the week the Partnership Council met, for example, the British government was rolling out a modest increase in the national minimum wage. That was good news as far as it went, delegates at the Odney Club agreed, but some wondered aloud about the virtues of a "living wage" rather than just a minimum wage, or even a "London living wage" for people working in the punishingly expensive capital. "We have a constitutional responsibility to pay partners for their performance," one delegate reminded his colleagues, as the group discussed the importance of "breaking the cycle of low pay" and the power of lifelong learning to move entry-level employees up the pay scale.

At that same meeting, there was also a calm, thorough, and businesslike review of changes to the pension plan, which, like many defined-benefit plans, was showing signs of long-term strain. Pensions had been a hot-button topic on this council for two years, perhaps the most potentially divisive issue it had worked on. A plan to create a hybrid defined benefit/defined contribution plan had been proposed, debated, revised, brought back to the partners, and debated again. In January, a few months after the October gathering, final revisions were approved unanimously, after a 51–11 vote not to delay any further. The vote "was an important moment for our democratic process," the company's 2015 Annual Report declared, as it confirmed the council's willingness to make such a big decision "in the best interests of the Partnership." Those are the

kinds of difficult choices that can be made openly and construc-
tively in an organization with a sense of shared fate and grassroots
participation, where nobody wins unless everybody wins.

"The focus of most companies is to improve their financial capital," argues Jane Burgess, the Partners' Counsellor. "Our focus is on
social capital. When people have a voice, when they feel like they
have influence, when they believe that they are fairly rewarded for
the contributions they make, it creates a sense of confidence in the
organization, and therefore more reasons to care about the organization and its future. Of course we need financial capital. But what
drives us forward is social capital."

The second visit that opened my eyes to the potential for big,
powerful organizations to share prosperity more widely was my
trip to Euclid, Ohio, on the south shore of Lake Erie. It was there, as
I previewed in the prologue, that I saw the robust social system
that sustains the competitive prowess of Lincoln Electric, a world-
class manufacturer of welding equipment and cutting machines
with annual sales of nearly $3 billion, some 10,000 employees, and
roughly 50 manufacturing facilities in 19 countries. The company
has been fiercely competitive, and consistently excellent, from the
day it was founded in 1895 by John C. Lincoln, with $200 and a plan
to build an electric motor he designed. Much of that excellence has
focused on quality, reliability, and, in recent years, all sorts of digital innovations that shape how its products (and thus the business)
perform. And it has performed. Lincoln Electric went public in
1995, one hundred years after it was established, and its stock has
soared by roughly 1,000 percent since then—genuinely impressive
results given the pressures and convulsions of the global markets
in which it operates.

Just as important to all this marketplace success, though, has been the company's history of workplace innovations that shape how its people perform and what their performance gets them. In 1914, Lincoln Electric established an Employee Advisory Board to give elected representatives a voice with senior management. In 1925, it created an ESOP through which rank-and-file workers owned stock and sold it back when they retired. It began its signature profit-sharing system in 1934, and its formal no-layoff pledge took shape in 1958. Meanwhile, almost from the beginning, and continuing to the present day, work at its flagship production complex in suburban Cleveland has been organized around a pay-for-performance system that measures individual productivity in exacting detail, compares the output of each employee with that of a peer group, and rewards people based on their results. Individual ratings also determine how big a bonus each employee receives, so star performers have a chance to benefit twice, with higher pay during the year and a larger bonus at the end of the year.

All these policies (and more) are the organizational legacy of James F. Lincoln, who ran the company from 1914 until his death in 1965, and they make Lincoln Electric what it is today—a tough, no-frills, fair-minded alternative to the corrosive toll of winner-take-all economics. Indeed, James Lincoln was to Lincoln Electric what Spedan Lewis was to the John Lewis Partnership: not the literal founder, but the founding father of the ideas and worldview that animate the enterprise. In the early days, for example, Lincoln would begin employee meetings with the greeting "Fellow workers"—about as collective and nonhierarchical as it gets. At the same time, he was a fanatic about personal motivation, which explains the company's rigorous pay-for-performance system. The result, more than one hundred years after he took charge, is that Lincoln Electric manages to foster both a fierce individual drive and a shared sense of purpose, to emphasize rigorous personal accountability, and to embrace a true shared identity.[11]

During our conversation at Lincoln Electric headquarters, I asked CEO Christopher Mapes whether James F. Lincoln would recognize the modern version of the company he built. "The social system would be very recognizable," Mapes assured me. "The Advisory Board, for example. I can't meet with the members every two weeks, like James Lincoln used to do, because a global business requires so much travel. But we meet every four or five weeks, the members are still elected by their peers, and we still post minutes for everyone to see. We have the same open-door policy, although employees are more likely to e-mail ahead of time to set up a meeting. So that culture of access is still here, it still resonates."

So too does the "culture of performance and productivity," Mapes continues, "because it's so foundational to what we do." Outside observers, he notes, often focus on the fact that the company puts thirty-two cents of every pretax dollar into a shared bonus pool. They also marvel at guaranteed employment, which Lincoln Electric maintained through the worst downturn since the Great Depression. "It sounds like 'We Are the World' stuff!" he jokes. "What people don't always see is that every day, you are measured on your performance. And every six months, you get a rating versus your peers. We are diligent about the ways we measure, analyze, and talk about individual performance. We ask everyone to give their best every day. But that only works if there's a mind-set that all of us are in the same game."

To be sure, Lincoln Electric is not a household name in the

United States in the way that John Lewis is in the United Kingdom. But it is, in its own way, an iconic organization. Its record of performance, fueled by its commitment to profit sharing and lifetime job security, has made it a subject of fascination for HR researchers, academics, and business-school students. In fact, a 1975 Harvard Business School case study, called, simply, "The Lincoln Electric Company," ranks among the bestselling HBS cases of all time. (Harvard has published at least six case studies and videos on the company since 1947, but the 1975 case has stayed at the top of the charts for forty years.)

Frank Koller, the former workplace correspondent for the Canadian Broadcasting Corporation, devoted an entire chapter to the case in his book *Spark*, a well-reported history of the company and its no-layoff pledge. The teaching note that accompanies the HBS case, Koller writes, reminds instructors that Lincoln Electric's model includes "significant obstacles" that other organizations might not be able to overcome. "But instructors are also reminded," he adds, "that the case is not about whether Lincoln's unusual approach *'might* work—it *has* worked, and very well.'"

"We ask everyone to give their best every day. But that only works if there's a mind-set that all of us are in the same game."

Norm Berg, the Harvard Business School professor who supervised the case study, reports that to this day, students have split reactions to the material. "The fundamental question about the

Lincoln Electric case study is to understand what induces or en-courages people to work hard, both in their own interests and in the interests of the company, and to do this on a continuing basis," he told Koller. "Some students will always say, 'It's perfect capitalism where workers have control over exactly what they do and get rewards based on their own efforts,' while others will say, 'This is practically a form of communism, not putting the stockholders first.'"

In the spirit of a business-school classroom, here's the key lesson I take away from the history of Lincoln Electric, and what that history suggests for the future of business and society: There is no inherent conflict between the zest for creativity and productivity, the unbridled spirit of enterprise that drives success, and a sense of fair play about who shares in that success. Quite the opposite: It may be harder to do business the Lincoln Electric way, but it's also more rewarding and sustainable. Organizations win bigger when they create opportunities for everyone to win.

Consider, for example, Lincoln Electric's much-admired no-lay-off pledge, which has held firm since 1958, and the pressures and choices the pledge imposes on senior management. Back in 2009, in the depths of the Great Recession, when Lincoln Electric saw 30 percent of its volume disappear in a single year, "We had discussions about whether or not we could maintain the guaranteed-employment policy," recalls CFO Vincent Petrella. "There was a lot of soul-searching. But we *had* to maintain it, it is such a part of who we are. This model requires much more management skill and expertise than hiring a thousand people when times are good, and whacking them when times get bad. It requires more active management."

It also requires, and creates, more engaged colleagues at every level. Doug Lance, senior vice president for North American operations, has spent twenty-five years with the company, all of them immersed in the inner workings of the plants. When I asked him what it takes for people to thrive in the Lincoln Electric social system, he replied, "a competitive fire; a will to win; do you have [the] drive to be the one on top?" But, he added, "competitive fire" has to be collective as well as personal. As a frontline worker, "I'm competing with everyone around me, I always want my individual performance to be better. At the same time we have to win as a team. The more the business achieves, the larger the profits. The larger the profits, the bigger the bonus pool."

It's hard to overestimate the impact of the annual bonus on what drives Lincoln Electric as an organization, and on the lives of its individual members. At John Lewis, the bonus is a nice way to end the year—in 2013, it represented a 15 percent boost to annual salaries. At Lincoln Electric, the bonus can be a make-or-break factor in people's financial well-being. In the boom year of 2013, the average bonus was a striking *70 percent* of annual base pay. For some highly rated employees, who, based on their peer rankings, receive far more than the average share of the pool, their end-of-year bonus payment was larger than their full-year base pay. (Lower-ranking employees, in turn, receive a smaller share of the bonus pool.) In the bust year of 2009, though, the bonus pool amounted to just 25 percent of total wages. Lean times, like good times, were shared by all.

That's why, every quarter, Vince Petrella posts a range of estimated outcomes for the so-called "bonus multiplier"—that is, high and low projections of how much the total bonus pool is expected to add to average base pay. Employees track the estimates closely, in part to plan their finances, but more to get a sense of what they can do to reach the high end by the end of the year. "Workers have the same thought processes as managers," the CFO emphasizes. "How can I improve productivity? How can I get rid of scrap? How can I drive performance in my unit?"

Meanwhile, on the second Friday of every December, CEO Chris Mapes gathers employees to reveal the size of the bonus pool, how it compares with prior years, the major business issues that drove it, and how all that relates back to the average bonus for every employee. "It allows us to congratulate everyone for their work," Mapes says, "and it encourages an ownership mind-set throughout the company. Everyone thinks about the business, because they *are* the business. It allows people to be an integral part of the improvement of the enterprise. We're in this together."

EPILOGUE:
WHAT'S YOUR STORY?

"Work Hard at Work Worth Doing"

More than a century ago, in his famous Square Deal speech to a Labor Day celebration in Syracuse, New York, President Theodore Roosevelt offered a definition of success that has stood the test of time. "Far and away the best prize that life offers," he said, "is the chance to work hard at work worth doing." In these times, "work worth doing" means work that elevates our sense of impact and enriches our sense of achievement—work that rewrites the story of success for a new era of business and leadership.

That has been the work of this book, which draws insights and lessons from organizations and leaders in a range of fields that are doing ordinary things in extraordinary ways. But these stories of success are valuable only if they contribute to *your* success, if they provide a set of ideas and a collection of practices that equip you to think bolder, aim higher, and win bigger. Here, then, is a distillation of the core messages of *Simply Brilliant*, eight questions whose answers, I hope, will help you to write a more rewarding story for yourself and the organizations you care about.

1. Can you develop a definition of success that allows you to stand apart from the competition and inspires others to stand with you?

What struck me about every organization and leader I chronicled in *Simply Brilliant* was the sense of purpose they exuded, and how that sense of purpose motivated colleagues, customers, and allies to contribute to their success. Brand strategist Adam Morgan calls it a "lighthouse identity"—a "very particular take" on what organizations are trying to achieve, a "compelling conviction" that their goals are "uniquely theirs" and uniquely important. Venture capitalist John Doerr prefers to invest in entrepreneurs who conduct themselves as "missionaries" as opposed to "mercenaries," founders who strive not just for success but for "success and significance."

The specifics of the metaphors are less important than the universality of the insight. The organizations and leaders that create the most value are the ones that position themselves as the most alluring alternative to a predictable (albeit efficient) status quo. Metro Bank's Vernon Hill likes to say, only half in jest, that he operates on the "lunatic fringe" of his industry—but that's precisely why so many employees and customers get so excited about something as mundane as retail banking. When I sat in on ISMs Day at Quicken Loans, a financial institution with no brick-and-mortar branches, founder Dan Gilbert made the same point. "We are zealots" about customer service, he told his colleagues, "we are on the lunatic fringe." This not is an argument for lunacy. But it *is* an argument for uniqueness and intensity: What do you do that other organizations can't or won't do?

2. Can you explain, clearly and compellingly, why what you do matters and how you expect to win?

Ultimately, the only sustainable form of leadership is thought leadership—championing an extraordinary set of ideas, not just good enough products and services. So leaders who think differently tend to talk differently as well. My *Fast Company* colleague and *Mavericks at Work* coauthor Polly LaBarre has observed that too many leaders communicate with "jargon monoxide"—empty rhetoric, mind-numbing buzzwords, eye-glazing acronyms. But the leaders we've encountered in *Simply Brilliant* are as precise with their words as they are creative with their ideas. They understand that they have to explain, in language that is unique to their field and compelling to the outside world, why what they do matters and how they expect to win.

When Rosanne Haggerty challenged her colleagues in the "homeless-industrial complex" to reimagine their strategies for addressing an intractable social problem, she led with a vigorous manifesto that spelled out the principles of the 100,000 Homes Campaign and invited others to come along. With precise and provocative language, she and her colleagues explained why they were breaking from convention in their field and how they expected to succeed. As I got to know Alaska's Southcentral Foundation and its remarkable work in health care, I kept tripping over the term "customer-owners," which holds a sacred place in the organization's vocabulary. "Can't I call people patients?" I pleaded. "Or customers?" But CEO Katherine Gottlieb was adamant. "We want people to live and breathe ownership of their health," she said, and to recognize that they literally own the health system that delivers care. That's why she and her colleagues talk the way they do. Do you know how to "talk the walk"?

3. Are you prepared to rethink the conventions of success in your field and the logic of your success as a leader?

The "paradox of expertise" is one of the most dangerous occupational hazards for leaders. In a world being remade before our eyes, leaders who make a difference are the ones who can rethink what's possible with their organizations. Yet the more closely you've looked at a field, and the longer you've been working and succeeding in it, the more difficult it can be to see new patterns, new prospects, new possibilities. The people with the most experience, knowledge, and resources in a particular area are often the last ones to seize opportunities for something dramatically new.

That's why this book devoted so much attention to leaders who were not just disrupting their industries but also disrupting themselves, leaders who, in the words of management thinker and jazz musician Frank J. Barrett, practice the art of "provocative competence." Barrett describes provocative competence as "leadership that enlivens activity and rouses the mind to life." I think of it more simply—as the capacity to reflect on your career, think hard about the future, and recognize that the mind-sets and skill sets that got you to where you are probably won't get you to where you want to go.

Robert Wennett, the boundlessly creative mind behind 1111 Lincoln Road, challenged almost every assumption in his field to build his one-of-a-kind parking structure and civic space in Miami's South Beach. Wennett took the disruptive ideas behind his creation so seriously, and so personally, that he decided to live in the structure he built. "People always ask me, 'Why would you choose to live in a parking garage?'" he cracks. "But the moment they walk in, they never ask again." How do you make sure that what you know doesn't limit what you can imagine?

4. Are you as determined to stay interested as to be interesting?

The most creative leaders I know are not just the boldest thinkers; they are the most insatiable learners. In his legendary speech on "Personal Renewal," John Gardner explored what it takes for leaders to stay relevant, effective, and engaged as they rise through the ranks. "Not anything as narrow as ambition," he said. "After all, ambition eventually wears out and probably should. But you can keep your zest until the day you die." Translation: As interesting as they may be, the most vital leaders figure out how to remain *interested*—in big ideas, in little surprises, in the enduring mission of their enterprise and all new ways to bring that mission to life.

Garry Ridge, CEO of WD-40, has built an organization filled with what he calls "learning maniacs." He and his colleagues have made an extraordinary commitment to maintain their "zest" for learning and discovery, to stay interested in new ideas about products and purpose even as they work to make the company and its brands more interesting to the outside world. He actually affixes an electronic signature to his e-mails with the message "Ancora

Imparo," Italian for "I am still learning"—a favorite phrase of Michelangelo's. "My dream," Ridge says, "is for this organization to be viewed as a leadership and learning laboratory for business." What's your strategy for personal renewal?

5. Do you pay as much attention to psychology and emotion as you do to technology and efficiency?

Nobody is opposed to a good deal—a dollars-and-cents value proposition that makes sense. But what we remember, what we appreciate, what we *prize*, are gestures of concern and compassion that introduce a touch of humanity into the all-too-bloodless calculations that define so much of modern life. In a world being reshaped by technology, what so many of us crave, what truly stand out, are small gestures of kindness that remind us of what it means to be human. As Mother Teresa famously advised: "Not all of us can do great things. But we can do small things with great love."

That's why leaders who aspire to do "great things" never lose sight of the small things that make such a huge impression inside and outside the organization. Pret A Manger, the fast-growing fast-casual British sandwich shop, works diligently to create an atmosphere of high energy and good cheer that generates what its CEO calls the Pret Buzz. Mercedes-Benz USA, which sells some of the best-designed automobiles on the planet, understands that extraordinary performance is as much about authentic emotion as it is about advanced engineering. "Every encounter with the brand," former CEO Stephen Cannon declares, "must be as extraordinary as the machine itself." Which means that all twenty-three thousand people who work for the company or at its dealerships must be "driven to delight" everyone they encounter. Are you trying to move products, or are you trying to move people?

6. Do the values that define how your organization works reflect the values proposition around which it competes?

The most successful companies I've studied don't just think differently from everyone else, they *care more* than everyone else— about the people they serve and the messages they send, about how everyone conducts themselves in a world with so many temptations to cut corners, fall back on procedure, and reward efficiency over empathy. You can't be special, distinctive, and exceptional in the marketplace unless you create something special, distinctive, and exceptional in the workplace. When it comes to "programming your culture," argues high-tech entrepreneur Ben Horowitz, the goal is to be "provocative enough to change what people do every day."

USAA, the financial-services juggernaut that does business with active and retired members of the U.S. military and their families, is so successful in the marketplace because it programs its culture so powerfully in the workplace. New employees eat MREs (Meals Ready to Eat) to get a taste for life on the front lines. They try on military backpacks and Kevlar vests, the better to appreciate the physical burdens soldiers carry with them. They read letters from soldiers to families and letters from families to soldiers. USAA immerses its employees, managers, and executives in the complex lives and emotional needs of the people they serve, so that everyone understands the level of connection to which the company aspires. Do you know how to elevate and energize how your

organization competes by elevating and energizing how your people behave?

7. Are you as humble as you are hungry?

If there's one lesson at the heart of the organizations chronicled
in *Simply Brilliant*, a perspective on success shared by leaders with
vastly different personalities, it's that exceptional performance begins with extraordinary insights. But that doesn't mean it's your
job to come up with those insights. In businesses (and social movements) built on new ideas, generating and evaluating ideas is everybody's business. That's why humility and ambition need not be
at odds. Indeed, humility *in the service of ambition* is the most effective mind-set for leaders who aspire to do big things in a world with
huge unknowns. As one CEO cited by Harvard Business School
leadership guru Linda Hill explained, "My job is to set the stage,
not perform on it."

In downtown Las Vegas, Zappos CEO Tony Hsieh is trying to
set the biggest stage imaginable, an entire urban neighborhood of
artists, entrepreneurs, geeks, and other creative types, none of
whom will work for his ecommerce company, but all of whom will
create "opportunities for serendipitous encounters" that can energize Zappos and fill it with new ideas. "The big bet is to get all these
different, diverse groups together in a relatively small space," Hsieh
has said, and "make sure they have a bias to collaborate." Can you
limit your ego to expand your creative horizon?

**8. Are you prepared to share the rewards of success with all
those who had a hand in achieving it?**

The "winner-take-all" model of success is not just an unsustainable way to organize a society; it's a lousy way to run a company. How can leaders summon their colleagues to rethink what's possible in their fields, to do things that others won't do, if they can't summon a sense that everyone is in it together? Internet evangelist Tim O'Reilly likes to say that successful companies "create more value than they capture." Put another way: The organizations that inspire the deepest sense of commitment in the ranks, and thus have a chance to make the biggest waves in the market, are the ones whose members get a seat at the table in terms of decision making and receive a fair share of the value they help to create.

The John Lewis Partnership, one of Great Britain's most admired retailers, is owned 100 percent in trust for its employees. To share the wealth, the partnership distributes a big chunk of its annual profits in a year-end bonus that is eagerly anticipated inside the company and widely reported on by the media. All ninety-four thousand employees vote in elections for colleagues to represent them in their local workplaces and at the highest levels of strategic deliberations. This full-fledged business democracy, complete with a written constitution, creates a sense of shared fate that has propelled the business forward. "The focus of most companies is to improve their financial capital," argues Jane Burgess, who oversees the democratic processes inside John Lewis. "Our focus is on social capital." Have you figured out how to give everyone in your organization a seat at the table and a piece of the action?

ACKNOWLEDGMENTS

Writing a book can be a lonely process—days, weeks, months hunched over a keyboard and cut off from outside distractions (well, other than Twitter and Facebook). Yet every other part of bringing a book to life, from conceiving the idea to delivering the proposal, from researching the material to clarifying the final arguments, is a group effort of the most rewarding kind. So I am pleased to acknowledge and thank those who played such an important role in the creation of *Simply Brilliant*.

Richard Pine of InkWell Management has been my literary agent for twenty-five years, but that does not begin to describe the role he plays in my literary career. Richard is the first person I call when I have an idea, the first person I hear from when I am falling behind, the best person I know to think through an argument, brainstorm a title, or revisit the organization of a manuscript. Truly, he does things that other literary agents can't or won't do, which is why he's the only agent for me. Thanks, Richard!

ACKNOWLEDGMENTS

This is the sixth book I've published in the last thirty years, and I've worked with some of the best-known publishing houses around. But I've never worked with a group that was as energetic, focused, committed—and, to be honest, intellectually demanding—as the talented folks at Portfolio. Niki Papadopoulos, my editor from the beginning of this project, put me through my paces in a way that no book editor has before—and, as a magazine editor myself, I can finally reveal now that I appreciated her high standards and insightful pushbacks, even if I had some dark nights of the soul along the way. Adrian Zackheim, Will Weisser, Leah Trouwborst, and everyone else at Portfolio has a keen eye for (and a clear point of view about) what it takes for a book like this to stand out in a crowded market. I love working with people with strong opinions, so I've loved working with the Portfolio team.

The digital team at *Harvard Business Review* gave me an outlet to test-drive some of my ideas in the early stages of researching this book, and to take a break with some short-form writing when the chapters began to drag. Thanks to Erica Truxler, Eric Hellweg, and the whole gang at *HBR* for providing me a platform when I had something to say and for leaving me alone when I went into hiding.

The lonely process of writing a book is just a prelude to the boisterous process of explaining it to a wider audience. For the last five years, the Washington Speakers Bureau has played an essential role in my ability to travel the world, participate in conferences and events, and share my messages with executives, entrepreneurs, community leaders, and so many interested and engaged audiences. I am grateful that the folks at WSB, who work with so many renowned leaders and thinkers, have been willing to represent me so strongly and treat me so well. To Nika Spencer, Kristin

ACKNOWLEDGMENTS

Downey, Christine Lancman, Annie Thalman, Sheldon Bream, and, of course, Christine Farrell, Harry Rhoads Jr., and everyone else at WSB—thanks for taking me into the fold and making me feel at home.

It's impossible to thank by name all the people at all the organizations who shared their experiences with me, provided information to me, and allowed me to visit factories and retail outposts, attend corporate events, even sit in on high-stakes meetings. (I did try to thank as many as I could in the footnotes.) I am always surprised, and eternally grateful, about how open busy and successful people can be with their time and insights. Their generosity throughout the research for this book was extraordinary.

And speaking of extraordinary . . . Chloe, Paige, and Grace continue to be the most supportive and inspiring family I could ask for. As anyone who's written a book knows all too well, every so often the emotional ups and downs call for a much-needed pat on the back, kick in the butt, or peck on the cheek. No one pats, kicks, and pecks better than you three.

NOTES

As I explain in the prologue, most of the material for this book comes from personal visits to the organizations I wrote about and interviews with senior leaders and associates at all levels of those organizations. Of course, I drew on many published sources (books, articles, academic research, business-school case studies) to provide background and context for my visits. These notes identify the material I found most valuable during the writing of *Simply Brilliant* and recognize the analysis and insights of the many professors, analysts, and journalists whose work informed my ideas.

PROLOGUE

1. See two columns in the *New York Times* by Thomas L. Friedman: "Average Is Over," January 24, 2012, and "Average Is Over, Part II," August 7, 2012. Those two columns drew on ideas Friedman had explored the year before in a well-received book. See Thomas L. Friedman and Michael Mandelbaum, *That Used to Be Us* (New York: Farrar, Straus and Giroux, 2011).
2. This quote from Lior Arussy comes from a personal conversation. But he has written a book that explores the same themes in greater depth. See

Lior Arussy, *Exceptionalize It!* (Hackensack, NJ: Strativity Group Inc., 2012).

3. See Marshall W. Meyer and Lynne G. Zucker, *Permanently Failing Organizations* (Thousand Oaks, CA: Sage Publications, 1989).

4. Linda Hill has written many books and articles worth reading. Start with Linda A. Hill and Kent Lineback, *Being the Boss: The 3 Imperatives for Becoming a Great Leader* (Boston: Harvard Business Review Press, 2011).

5. John W. Gardner's discussion of "tough optimism" comes from a speech titled "Personal Renewal" delivered to McKinsey & Company. You can find it online at pbs.org/johngardner/sections/writings_speech_1.html.

CHAPTER 1

1. Francis Tibbalds, "Milton Keynes—Who Forgot the Urban Design?" *Places* 1, no. 4 (1984).

2. Most of my insights on Metro Bank come from personal visits to the bank's London headquarters and Milton Keynes store, interviews with senior executives, and years' worth of conversations with Vernon Hill. That said, a few print sources were important. See Shawn Tully, "Vernon Hill Is the Best Damn Banker Alive (Just Ask Him)," *Fortune*, September 15, 2010; and John Engen, "Vernon Hill on the Wooing of Customers in London," *American Banker*, December 1, 2012.

3. "A Report on the Culture of British Retail Banking," New City Agenda and Cass Business School, 2014, http://newcityagenda.co.uk/wp-con tent/uploads/2014/11/Online-version.pdf.

4. Polly LaBarre and I wrote about Commerce Bank in *Mavericks at Work: Why the Most Original Minds in Business Win* (New York: William Morrow, 2006).

5. Sadly, about ten months after I met Sir Duffield in Milton Keynes, he passed away at the advanced age of thirteen. Vernon and Shirley Hill distributed a lovely tribute to Duffy's role as the bank's mascot. "We will miss him," they wrote, "but he will live forever as part of Metro Bank's history." They also announced that they had adopted a fourteen-week-

old puppy from the same bloodline as Duffy as his successor. His name: Sir Duffield II.

6. Michael Lanning has written extensively (and influentially) on the value proposition. See, for example, Michael J. Lanning and Edward G. Michaels, "A Business Is a Value Delivery System," *McKinsey Quarterly*, June 2000; and his book, *Delivering Profitable Value* (New York: Basic Books, 1998).

7. Again, this insight came from a personal interview. But see also Lior Arussy, *Exceptionalize It!*

8. Adam Morgan and his colleagues are some of the smartest (and most prolific) brand strategists I know. Start with Adam Morgan, *Eating the Big Fish: How Challenger Brands Can Compete Against Brand Leaders* (Hoboken, NJ: John Wiley, 2009).

9. Sadly, I did not have the chance to visit Helsinki during my research for the book. However, I got an extensive update on SOL from Juhapekka Joronen, Liisa Joronen's son, who now runs a big chunk of the business. My writing on SOL draws from this interview along with two essential print sources: Gina Imperato, "Dirty Business, Bright Ideas," *Fast Company*, March 1997; and Brian M. Carney and Isaac Getz, *Freedom, Inc.* (New York: Crown Business, 2009), which has a fascinating chapter on the company.

10. The most accessible introduction to Gregory Treverton's thinking is Gregory F. Treverton, "Risks and Riddles," *Smithsonian*, June 2007. Malcolm Gladwell wrote about Treverton's ideas in his analysis of the mysterious demise of Enron. See "Open Secrets," *New Yorker*, January 8, 2007.

CHAPTER 2

1. The story about Tim Cook appears in Adam Lashinsky, *Inside Apple: How America's Most Admired—and Secretive—Company Really Works* (New York: Business Plus, 2012).

2. See Simon Sinek, *Start with Why: How Great Leaders Inspire Everyone to Take Action* (New York: Portfolio, 2009).

3. John Doerr has given several in-depth presentations at Stanford Business School on the nature of entrepreneurship. See "Entrepreneurs Are Missionaries," April 4, 2007, www.youtube.com/watch?v=n6iwEYmbCwk; and "What It Takes to Be a Remarkable Leader," November 19, 2009, you tube.com/watch?v=LDWURusr02k.

4. See Randy Komisar, *The Monk and the Riddle* (Boston: Harvard Business Review Press, 2000). In the spring of 2015, Randy Komisar and John Doerr figured prominently in a sexual-discrimination lawsuit filed by Ellen Pao, a former colleague of theirs at the VC firm. Although Kleiner Perkins won the case on all counts, the trial left the firm, Doerr, Komisar, and all of Silicon Valley, for that matter, uncomfortable and embarrassed about the macho culture of high tech. I can't speak to the details of the case, but it should not diminish Kleiner's legacy as a pioneer in the venture-capital field and the power of Doerr's insights as an investor and a company builder.

5. My friend and *Fast Company* cofounder Alan Webber tells the Bill Graham story in *Rules of Thumb: 52 Truths for Winning at Business Without Losing Your Self* (New York: Harper Business, 2009). For a real trip, see Barry Barnes, *Everything I Know About Business I Learned from the Grateful Dead* (New York: Business Plus, 2011). For an in-depth and moving report on the Fare Thee Well tour, see Jon Pareles, "Review: No Song Left Unsung, Grateful Dead Plays Its Last," *New York Times*, July 6, 2015.

6. Thanks to Pal's Sudden Service for allowing me to audit classes at the Pal's Business Excellence Institute. There have been several good articles written about the company. Two of the best are Leigh Buchanan, "Training the Best Damn Fry Cooks (and Future Leaders) in the U.S.," April 23, 2014, inc.com; and "Pal's: America's Least-Known Well-Run Burger Chain," July 2, 2012, burgerbusiness.com.

7. Thanks to Aaron Emerson, vice president of communications at Quicken Loans, for hosting an intense and eye-opening visit to ISMs in Action and to company headquarters. What I saw during my time in Detroit informs most of what I wrote, although a few print sources were

important as background information. See especially Tim Alberta, "Is Dan Gilbert Detroit's New Superhero?" *National Journal*, February 27, 2014; David Segal, "A Missionary's Quest to Remake Motor City," *New York Times*, April 13, 2013; and Amanda Lewan, "Quicken Loans Innovates with a 'Small Business' Culture," michipreneur.com, March 5, 2013.

CHAPTER 3

1. My analysis of the work of Rosanne Haggerty and her colleagues draws mainly on personal interviews with her, Becky Margiotta, Joe McCannon, and other advisers to the 100,000 Homes Campaign, as well as my participation in the New Haven canvass. But I relied on other sources as well. Haggerty's presentation to the BIF-9 Collaborative Innovation Summit is a brilliant distillation of her career (youtube.com/watch?v=Y1Sn4x-GiR-Y). Also important were Alastair Gordon, "Higher Ground," *Wall Street Journal*, June 10, 2012; and a business-school case study, Professor Howard Yu, "Finding Community Solutions from Common Ground: A New Business Model to End America's Homelessness," IMD, 2013.

2. See Cynthia Barton Rabe, *The Innovation Killer: How What We Know Limits What We Can Imagine—and What Smart Companies Are Doing About It* (New York: AMACOM, 2006). This book has had a huge impact on how I think about making change in big companies. I want to take a moment to pay tribute to Cynthia Barton Rabe, who, tragically, was killed by a hit-and-run driver behind the wheel of a stolen car. She was just forty-seven years old.

3. I did not get a chance to participate in Amy Herman's Art of Perception seminar, but there have been several excellent write-ups of her work. See especially Neal Hirschfeld, "Teaching Cops to See," *Smithsonian*, October 2009; Ellen Byron, "To Master the Art of Solving Crimes, Cops Study Vermeer," *Wall Street Journal*, July 27, 2005; and Leslie Berger, "By Observing Art, Med Students Learn Art of Observation," *New York Times*, January 2, 2001.

4. Thanks to Michael Fassnacht and his colleagues at FCB Chicago for hosting me and sharing their ideas, methodologies, and workbooks.

5. Frank J. Barrett has been writing about "provocative competence" for more than a decade. The best source of his thinking is Frank J. Barrett, *Yes to the Mess: Surprising Leadership Lessons from Jazz*, (Boston: Harvard Business Review Press, 2012).

6. See Michael Barbaro, "A Miami Beach Event Space. Parking Space, Too," *New York Times*, January 23, 2011. The short film, called *eleven eleven*, produced by Elizabeth Priore, is online at http://vimeo.com/groups/fo cusforwardfilms/videos/51889050.

CHAPTER 4

1. Dennis K. Berman, "Is Peanut Butter Pop-Tart an Innovation?" *Wall Street Journal*, December 3, 2013. See also Bill Taylor, "Stop Me Before I 'Innovate' Again!" HBR.org, December 6, 2013.

2. See Mihaly Csikszentmihalyi, *Creativity: The Psychology of Discovery and Invention* (New York: Harper Perennial, 2013).

3. My analysis of Megabus is based largely on my interviews in Paramus, New Jersey, with Dale Moser, Mike Alvich, and Bryony Chamberlain. Another key source was Ben Austen, "The Megabus Effect," *Bloomberg Businessweek*, April 7, 2011.

4. You can find John W. Gardner's speech on "Personal Renewal" at pbs.org/johngardner/sections/writings_speech_1.html.

5. Roy Spence, *The 10 Essential Hugs of Life* (Austin, TX: Greenleaf Book Group Press, 2014).

6. My analysis of WD-40 is based largely on personal interviews with Garry Ridge and Graham Milner. But I did rely on print sources as well. See especially Jay Palmer, "The Cult of WD-40," *Barron's*, December 3, 2001; and Jonathan Horn, "WD-40: Rust Free After 60 Years," *San Diego Union-Tribune*, September 14, 2013.

CHAPTER 5

1. The best way to understand the work of Southcentral Foundation is to visit Anchorage and spend time with its leaders and frontline personnel, which I was lucky to do. For background and supporting analysis, I did rely on a number of sources. Here is the material I found most valuable: Erin E. Sullivan and Theodore Hufstader, "Human Systems for Southcentral Foundation's Nuka System of Care" (parts A and B), Harvard Medical School Center for Primary Care, 2015; "Nuka System of Care: Our Transformation," presentation by Douglas Eby and Leanndra Ross, Asia-Pacific Healthcare Conference, September 2, 2014; Katherine Gottlieb, "The Nuka System of Care: Improving Health Through Ownership and Relationships," *International Journal of Circumpolar Health*, 2013; "A Formula for Cutting Health Costs," *New York Times*, July 21, 2012.
2. See Tim Nudd, "How a Fan Post on Panera's Facebook Page Got Half a Million Likes," *Adweek*, August 14, 2012. See also Bill Taylor, "It's More Important to Be Kind Than Clever," HBR.org, August 23, 2012.
3. I first wrote about my father's Buick for *HBR*. See "Why Is It So Hard to Be Kind?" HBR.org, October 19, 2010.
4. Andrew E. Kramer, "Russian Service, and with Please and Thank You," *New York Times*, November 1, 2013.
5. I've been following Pret A Manger since we first wrote about it in *Fast Company*. See Scott Kirsner, "Recipe for Reinvention," *Fast Company*, April 2002. As for the hue and cry over its commitment to friendly service, this collection of articles captures the debate: Stephanie Clifford, "Would You Like a Smile with That?" *New York Times*, August 6, 2011; Richard Preston, "Smiley Culture: Pret A Manger's Secret Ingredients," *Telegraph*, March 9, 2012; Paul Myerscough, "Short Cuts," *London Review of Books*, January 2013; Timothy Noah, "Labor of Love," *New Republic*, February 1, 2013. See also Bill Taylor, "Pret a Manger Wants Happy Employees—That's Okay," HBR.org, November 7, 2013.
6. See the e-book Ward Clapham, *Breaking With the Law: The Story of Positive Tickets*, June 1, 2010, available on Amazon.com.

7. For the Jeff Bezos speech, see "We Are What We Choose," baccalaureate remarks as delivered to the Princeton University Class of 2010 by Jeff Bezos, May 30, 2010. For the *New York Times* investigation, see Jodi Kantor and David Streitfeld, "Inside Amazon: Wrestling Big Ideas in a Bruising Workplace," *New York Times*, August 15, 2015. Details on the Amazon.love memo can be found in Brad Stone, *The Everything Store: Jeff Bezos and the Age of Amazon* (New York: Little, Brown and Company, 2013).

CHAPTER 6

1. See Kevin Roberts, *Lovemarks: The Future Beyond Brands* (New York: powerHouse Books, 2005); and Kevin Roberts, *The Lovemarks Effect: Winning in the Consumer Revolution* (New York: powerHouse Books, 2006).

2. I have been a student of USAA since my days as a young editor at *HBR*, when we published an interview with its long-serving (and legendary) CEO, General Robert McDermott. This collection of articles provides a good overview of the company's remarkable growth: Thomas Teal, "Service Comes First: An Interview with Robert F. McDermott," *Harvard Business Review*, September 1991; Jena McGregor, "USAA's Battle Plan," *Bloomberg Businessweek*, February 18, 2012; Kristina Shevory, "Boot Camp for Bankers," *New York Times*, September 1, 2014; Jenna Hiller, "USAA Employees Experience Basic Training at 'Zero Day,'" KSAT.com, July 22, 2013.

3. For brilliant riffs on strategy, culture, and all sorts of other topics, see Ben Horowitz, *The Hard Thing About Hard Things: Building a Business When There Are No Easy Answers* (New York: Harper Business, 2014).

4. Thanks to Stephen Cannon for allowing me to sit in on his presentation to the Forrester Forum, "Why Good Enough Is Not Good Enough," June 24, 2014. My account of the changes at Mercedes-Benz USA is based on personal conversations with Cannon, Harry Hynekamp, and Lior Arussy. (As of January 1, 2016, Stephen Cannon became CEO of the AMB Group, parent company of the Atlanta Falcons.) After I completed this manuscript, a book-length treatment of the Mercedes-Benz USA journey

was published. See Joseph A. Michelli, *Driven to Delight* (New York: Mc-Graw-Hill Education, 2016).

CHAPTER 7

1. Tony Hsieh's Downtown Project has attracted elaborate press coverage, some of it celebratory, some of it critical, much of it valuable. In addition to my visits to both Zappos and the Downtown Project, and several in-depth conversations with Hsieh, I drew on a handful of especially good articles. See Susan Berfield, "Hard Times in Happy Town," *Bloomberg Businessweek*, December 29, 2014; Colin Marshall, "Downtown and Out? The Truth About Tony Hsieh's $350m Las Vegas Project," *Guardian*, November 20, 2014; Sara Corbett, "How Zappos' CEO Turned Las Vegas into a Startup Fantasyland," *Wired*, January 1, 2014; Timothy Pratt, "What Happens in Brooklyn Moves to Las Vegas," *New York Times Magazine*, October 19, 2012. See also Re/code's online series about the Downtown Project at http://recode.net/tag/downtown-project/. For a look at holacracy inside Zappos, see Jerry Useem, "Are Bosses Necessary?" *Atlantic*, October 2015.

2. See Edward Glaeser, *Triumph of the City: How Our Greatest Invention Makes Us Richer, Smarter, Greener, Healthier, and Happier* (New York: Penguin Press, 2011).

3. Tony Hsieh has spoken extensively on the ideas that have shaped the Downtown Project. See, for example, his address to the BIF-8 Summit hosted by the Business Innovation Factory in September 2012 (https://www.youtube.com/watch?v=lU1H1GyWCQA). See also "The City as Startup," his address to the South by Southwest V2V conference in August 2013 (https://www.youtube.com/watch?v=aYjv4dKl7OM). My quotes from him in this chapter draw from both personal conversations as well as these public speeches.

4. See Andrea Chang, "After Jody Sherman Death, Tech Community Seeks Dialogue on Suicide," *Los Angeles Times*, February 1, 2013.

5. See Kristy Totten, "Living Small: At Downtown's Airstream Park, Home Is Where the Experiment Is," *Las Vegas Weekly*, February 5, 2015. For a

meticulously detailed report on Tony Hsieh's mind-bending innovations at Zappos and in Downtown Las Vegas, see Roger D. Hodge, "First, Let's Get Rid of All the Bosses," *New Republic*, October 2015.

6. See Linda A. Hill, Greg Brandeau, Emily Truelove, and Kent Lineback, *Collective Genius* (Boston: Harvard Business Review Press, 2014); and Linda Hill, "Leading from Behind," HBR.org, May 5, 2010.

7. I have been learning from and writing about the endlessly creative Rob McEwen for more than a decade. For more details on his history at Goldcorp and the story of the Goldcorp Challenge, see Linda Tischler, "He Struck Gold on the Net (Really)," *Fast Company*, June 2002; and William C. Taylor and Polly LaBarre, *Mavericks at Work: Why the Most Original Minds in Business Win* (New York: William Morrow, 2006).

8. See Edgar H. Schein, *Humble Inquiry: The Gentle Art of Asking Instead of Telling* (San Francisco: Berrett-Koehler Publishers, 2013).

9. See Gary Hamel, *What Matters Now: How to Win in a World of Relentless Change, Ferocious Competition, and Unstoppable Innovation* (San Francisco: Jossey-Bass, 2012).

10. Thanks to Jean DuBois at Fastenal, who organized an eye-opening (and exhausting) visit to the company, its facilities, and even its newly opened museum. Thanks as well to all the Fastenal people, from senior executives to warehouse managers, who took the time to explain the inner workings of this remarkable organization. For background information on Fastenal, see Robert Farzad, "Fastenal's Runaway Stock Success," *Bloomberg Businessweek*, February 27 to March 4, 2012; and Dyan Machan, "Fastenal's CEO Sweats the Small Stuff," *Barron's*, March 8, 2014.

CHAPTER 8

1. The time I spent at the Odney Club with the John Lewis Partnership allowed me to see organizational democracy in action, and to interview both high-level executives and frontline contributors. In addition to these conversations, a few print sources were important sources of history and background information. See Peter Cox, *Spedan's Partnership:*

The Story of John Lewis and Waitrose (London: Labatie Books, 2010); and Michael Skapinker and Andrea Felsted, "John Lewis: Trouble in Store," *Financial Times*, October 16, 2015.

2. The constitution of the John Lewis Partnership is available online, as is a treasure trove of information and explanations of the organization's business results and democratic practices. Visit johnlewispartnership .co.uk.

3. See Tamsin Blanchard, "John Lewis Turns 150: The Story of a Very Civil Partnership," *Telegraph*, April 19, 2014.

4. Jacob S. Hacker and Paul Pierson, *Winner-Take-All Politics: How Washington Made the Rich Richer—and Turned Its Back on the Middle Class* (New York: Simon & Schuster, 2010).

5. Sylvia A. Allegretto, Ken Jacobs, Dave Graham-Squire, and Megan Emiko Scott, "The Public Cost of Low-Wage Jobs in the Banking Industry," UC Berkeley Labor Center, October 2014.

6. See Bonnie Brown, *Giigle: How I Got Lucky Massaging Google* (Dallas: Highland Loch Press, 2012).

7. "Turning Workers into Capitalists," *Economist*, November 25, 2013.

8. Polly LaBarre and I first wrote about Dick Resch and KI in *Mavericks at Work*. I conducted new interviews with Dick Resch and other KI executives in the summer of 2015 to get updates on the company's performance and the evolution of the concept of "social capitalism."

9. I first wrote about Cecil Ursprung and Reflexite in "These Workers Act Like Owners (Because They Are)," *New York Times*, May 21, 2006. I conducted further interviews with Ursprung in mid-2015 to explore the sale of the company and how employees fared as a result.

10. Alex Ralph, "John Lewis Bonus Likely to Be Reduced," *Times* (London), March 9, 2015.

11. My sincere thanks to Amanda Butler of Lincoln Electric for organizing a fabulous visit to Euclid, Ohio. My thoughts on the company were shaped mainly by the many in-person interviews I conducted, but some published sources were important as well. See Frank Koller, *Spark: How Old-Fashioned Values Drive a Twenty-First-Century Corporation* (New

York: PublicAffairs, 2010); and Norman Fast, under the direction of Professor Norman Berg, "The Lincoln Electric Company," Harvard Business School Case 9-376-028, 1975. See also William Serrin, "The Way That Works at Lincoln," *New York Times*, January 15, 1984; and Barnaby J. Feder, "Rethinking a Model Incentive Plan," *New York Times*, September 5, 1994.

INDEX

INDEX

INDEX

INDEX

INDEX